The Adventures of Mr.Brightside

Ryan Jacobson

To my loving parents, William and Michelle Jacobson, without which there would likely be no book, probably be no venture, and unequivocally be no me.

"Dream as if you'll live forever. Live as if you'll die today."

- James Dean

"Come on in, guys."

- Jeff Probst, *Survivor*

Table of Contents

Prologue - Venture Twelve - 7

1. Azores Low - The Venture Begins - 12
2. Azores Moderate - Azorean Parade Madness - 17
3. Azores High - Unsolved Mystery at Luxury Resort - 25

4. Morocco Low - The Snake Swindler - 33
5. Morocco Moderate - The Horrible Hagglers - 39
6. Morocco High - Desert Decadence - 45

7. Albania Low - The Hills Are Alive With the Sound of Fighting - 56
8. Albania Moderate - Does Anyone Want to go to Montenegro? - 61
9. Albania High - Albanian Jackpot - 69

10. India Low - A Warm Indian Welcome - 81
11. India Moderate - The Holiest High - 94
12. India High - I Told You This Wasn't a Good Idea - 106

13. Sri Lanka Low - Catch of the Day - 113
14. Sri Lanka Moderate - Bloody Tea Time - 125
15. Sri Lanka High - Safari Slap - 132

16. Thailand Low - Fire in the Sky - 140
17. Thailand Moderate - The Life of Pai - 147
18. Thailand High - Finding Mr. Brightside - 153

19. Laos Low - In a Barbie World - 163
20. Laos Moderate - The Slow (Love) Boat - 170
21. Laos High - WaterFALL Disaster - 177

22. Cuba Low - Rum'ing in the Rain - 184
23. Cuba Moderate - Hemingway's Paparazzi - 191
24. Cuba High - Luxury Ride to Nowhere - 201

25. Mexico Low - World Wonder Tour Guide - 209
26. Mexico Moderate - Sticking Out Like a Sore Yogi - 213
27. Mexico High - No Such Thing as a Free Meal - 221

28. Belize Low - Death by Lionfish - 232
29. Belize Moderate - Death By Stingray - 237
30. Belize High - Death By Hell's Itch - 244

31. Panama Low - Good Dry-Day - 250
32. Panama Moderate - The Sole Survivor - 259
33. Panama High - Cartagena's Game of Thrones - 270

34. Peru Low - Does Anyone Want Anything? - 278
35. Peru Moderate - I'm Ziplining, Baby! - 287
36. Peru High - The Final Venture - 302

Aknowledgements - 315

* To view pictures of all the events you're about to read, follow along at www.venturetwelve.com/the-book

Prologue
Venture Twelve

The cuttlefish is an astonishing animal. It has the fascinating ability to effortlessly blend into any environment it needs. The cuttlefish can instantly change its color, shape, or movement, all at once if need be, to communicate or camouflage.

From birth, the cuttlefish can already display at least 13 different types of body patterns, and miraculously are born with the unique ability to turn into whatever it requires in order to survive.

They have enormously large brains in relation to their body which enables them to learn and remember. And despite being colorblind, have exceptional eyesight. The fact that they are COLORBLIND and can still morph into any shade of any color they need to instantaneously, is nothing short of a mind-blowing feat of nature.

As a child in the eighties, I always would get obsessive about our upcoming family vacations. With no internet to research new places or adventures, I would read brochures from cover to cover, circling everything that my 7-year-old brain determined was a "must-visit" attraction, and unapologetically slashing a violent, dark "X" across anything that I deemed would be too boring for my self-diagnosed ADD brain to handle. Sorry Mom, Dad and older brother Cory, those boring things are off-limits. This is MY vacation.

Our family would typically take biennial trips to Walt Disney World, and for months prior to the trip, I would compulsively watch the same *Disney Vacation* planning video over and over again until, eventually, I would ruin the VHS.

To say I was a vacation planning nerd is an understatement.

I loved exploring new places (as long as there was a gift shop) and I loved trying new things (as long as it wasn't the slightest bit boring or educational.) I have always had this side of me that wanted to see and do as much as possible in my life, and that desire, nearly thirty years after disintegrating the Big Red Boat - Disney Cruise Line information magazine due to overuse, has led me to this venture around the world.

The original idea for this journey was that it would become a project called *Venture Twelve,* in which I would attempt to travel around the world for 12 months, exploring 12 countries, all while spending only 12 thousand dollars.

After crunching some numbers while sipping a martini in my parents' hot tub, both myself and my family immediately realized that someone like me, who is known for an uncanny ability to enjoy the finer things in life when it comes to traveling, could never survive on one thousand dollars a month while traveling around the world.

So I went back to the drawing board.

While it is true that I enjoy the finer things in life, I do also have the ability to "rough it," and get down and dirty.

I have spent a week hiking the Grand Canyon, showering exactly zero times along the way and literally sleeping on a picnic table at the bottom. But I have also spent a week getting VIP tours and access to some of the best vineyards and wineries in Napa Valley, Bordeaux, and Stellenbosch.

I have spent a summer in the war-torn area of Gulu, Uganda working in schools for children affected by the Lord's Resistance Army led by Joseph Kony. I would ride a Boda Boda on the back of a Ugandan man every day for a half-hour each way, only to arrive at the school covered in red dirt from head to toe. I would go to dinner with no electricity in the pitch dark, only using fading, dim headlamps and the ability to feel for our food, picking it up with our hands and eating it, not knowing what it was, or where it came from. I would sleep in a small room, with two twin mattresses, mosquito nets and a nightstand that I shared with my roommate Michael. Outside our room, was a 6'7" Ugandan soldier holding an AK-47. What he was protecting us from, I never asked. I didn't want to know the answer.

But I have also mingled with celebrities at parties in LA and got drunk, alone, with Justin Timberlake in a speakeasy at a mansion in Connecticut.

The point is, I am like a cuttlefish. I have the ability to blend into any environment I need to in order to survive whatever situation I find myself randomly landing.

At least I thought I did before I began this adventure.

So this was a test. The old format of *Venture Twelve* was thrown out the window and replaced with the new format. It would still be called *Venture Twelve,* but this time, I would spend 12 days in every country that I went to. But there was a catch.

- The first four days would be spent living on a very low budget. I would stay at hostels, or campgrounds, or anything else that was in line with a very tight, backpackers' budget. I would eat street food, or find cheap local food, or even cook my own meals indigenous to the area. And I would spend relatively no money on entertainment or activities. I would do free sightseeing tours, or explore towns or cities on my own. I would wander aimlessly, getting lost at each destination and enjoying its beauty all while spending hardly any money.

- The next four days I would stay in the same country, but typically move to a new city. I would spend days five through eight living on a moderate budget. I would stay at moderately priced hotels, or lodges. I would eat at decent restaurants, or shops. And I would have a middling budget to spend on any activities or adventures that I wanted to experience in the region.

- My final four days in a country I would live on an all-out luxury budget. I would stay at the nicest resorts, dine at the fanciest restaurants, and have no reservations about spending money on activities or excursions. I would live like a king.

Then, after I have fully explored the destination on all budget levels, I would make my way to the next destination and start the process all over again. For an entire year.

There is something about going from being pampered at a five-star resort to getting the top bunk in a room full of eleven strangers the very next day that is, to say the very least, humbling.

At thirty-eight years old was I too old to fit into hostel life with two full designer suits in my luggage? Did I lack the ability to blend into some of the best restaurants in the world a few days after eating a scorpion on the side of the road in Bangkok? Was I too immature to commingle in five-star resorts and spas without overindulging on their free champagne service?

Spoiler alert: The answer to all of those questions is a resounding "YES!"

But, like the cuttlefish, I was going to do my damndest to instantly, and effortlessly blend into whatever environment I needed to in order to communicate, camouflage and survive.

The cuttlefish, when feeling threatened, will release a black ink from their bodies, distracting their predators from their whereabouts and ensuring they have time to flee, or properly camouflage themselves.

This ink was once used by writers and artists and still used today in many fine-dining dishes around the world.

As a traveler and writer, then, I will channel my inner cuttlefish when my social skills are simply not enough to allow me to blend into these vastly different cultures I will be submerging myself in. So when I begin to feel threatened, and like I can no longer blend in I will release my ink.

I will whip out my ink and write.

1. Azores, Portugal
Low Budget
The Venture Begins

It was my own fault. If I had not insisted on buying the strangers next to me on my flight to the Azores a beer upon arrival, I would not have been in this situation. I would have made it to the camp at 7:00 p.m., the time they were expecting me, and were waiting patiently for my arrival in order to give me the customary welcome tour of the phenomenal Banana Eco Camp on the Azorean island of Terceira.

I *should* have been resting comfortably in my cozy little teepee log cabin, and reflecting peacefully on the first day of my adventure around the world. Maybe I would have shared my first meal with my camp neighbors, or perhaps opened a bottle of wine with the owners as a celebratory offering because they were my first of many stops around the world. And I almost certainly would have joined in for a few sing-along campfire songs, while asking everyone in sight with a guitar if they knew how to play "Mr. Brightside" by The Killers. Because if there is one thing in this world that I am good at, it is singing "Mr. Brightside" by The Killers, but I digress.

But I wasn't sitting around a campfire, or settling into my new teepee cabin for the next four nights. I was at an airport bar, basically holding two strangers captive and forcing them to commemorate the fact that they were my first "friends" that I made on the year-long *Venture Twelve* project.

So, needless to say, I was late. Multiple hours late.

As soon as the taxi drove down the long, narrow, and dark dirt road heading towards the closed gates of the camp, I knew that I had made a big mistake. After pounding on the gates for what seemed like hours (thanks in part to those celebratory beers I had to have) an off duty employee opens the gate only to find a disheveled, buzzed American with enough luggage to fill an 18 wheeler.

"Hi, I am Ryan… the writer from America. I am staying here," is close enough to the words that I probably uttered.

"You're very late," replied the worker, who I more than likely unceremoniously awoke with my banging on the gate (along with the rest of the campers, who are clearly way more responsible than me, and were tucked neatly into their sleeping bags or beds way before my grand entrance.)

"I would give you the tour now, but it will be best if we hold off until tomorrow, you know, so you can actually *see* what I am showing you, and so we will not wake any of the campers that you haven't already startled half to death," said the very friendly, yet stern older gentleman.

"That's *totally* fine," I said, as I was in no condition to be led on a tour after an international flight and multiple beers anyway.

"Oh, and you're going to have to sleep in a tent tonight, because the owners already went home, and you were not here in order for them to give you the key to your teepee cabin."

"Sure, no problem at all!" I managed to exclaim in my most overly-dramatic positive tone, almost as if I was a pep rally cheerleader. But inside I was desperately trying to hide the panic in my voice that I was going to have to attempt to assemble a tent while buzzed, all on my own at nearly midnight, in a banana plant jungle.

I am a lot of things, but a manly man is not one of them. If you want to laugh your ass off for hours on end, ask me to assemble a tent by myself… or start a fire… or change the oil in my car… or kill a spider… or know what the hell a wrench is.

So you can imagine my relief when the poor man that was sleeping just minutes prior, and now was forced to converse with some strange American man, tells me there is an extra tent they set up for me way over in the banana fields and I can sleep there for the night. "Tomorrow morning when you get up," he said, "You can move into my new fancy teepee cabin."

More like when I get up tomorrow LATE afternoon, I said under my breath, because of my uncanny ability of sleeping in.

So there I am, too tired to unpack and lying fully clothed in a tent. I am in the middle of a banana plant jungle, in the middle of an Azorean island, in the middle of the Atlantic Ocean. I know exactly zero people on the island except for a man that very likely hates me. My two "best airplane friends" that I insisted on making, were only there for a few hour layover before heading off to Lisbon.

I have no sleeping bag, no pillow, and all my electronic devices are dead. It's day one and I already misplaced the

$75 headlamp that I deemed a vital purchase before the trip, so I couldn't even read a book. But I did have some entertainment because the constant battle of killing mosquitoes before they bit me kept me plenty entertained for a few hours as my head slid deeper and deeper into a ditch at the end of the tent. Despite all this, I managed to doze off to sleep for a few minutes before being stirred awake by the sound of rain. I awoke even further once the rain started dripping into the tent. Then dripping all over my face, all over my clothes, and all over my luggage. Basically all over my life.

And to think, just 12 hours earlier I was in my home, with everyone I love. My family and friends not only had a killer going away party for me, but my cousins Rachel and Sean also suggested we hire a party bus to take me on the hour and a half journey to Logan Airport in Boston, MA to get my venture started the right way.

Never have I regretted anything more in my life than in this moment. Why did I leave my perfect life back home? I left a great job, amazing friends, a loving, supportive family, and perhaps most importantly, a very comfortable bed, to travel around the world all by myself.

Between physically slapping myself to avoid getting a mosquito-borne illness on day one and mentally beating the crap out of myself for up and leaving the life I loved at home, I am not ashamed to admit that I shed a few tears that first night in the Azores; the first night of my venture around the world.

But I made myself a promise that night… that this would be the only night I would allow myself to feel this way. This is the saddest, most doubtful, most pessimistic, and most scared I will be all year.

Tomorrow I will wake up and I will be a new man. Tomorrow I will wake up and be ready to see the world. Tomorrow I will get up and explore. Tomorrow I will apologize to my neighbors for walking them up at midnight with my yells of "Hey! I am Ryan, can someone open the gate." Tomorrow I will wake up and become the travel writer that I have always wanted to be. Tomorrow I will wake up and my life will change forever.

Just not until like at least noon. I really, really am not a morning person.

2. Azores, Portugal
Moderate Budget
Azorean Parade Madness

Every year in Ponta Delgada, on the island of Sao Miguel, there is a four-day celebration at the beginning of July called the Grandes Festas do Divino Espírito Santo de Ponta Delgada (Great Festivities of the Divine Holy Spirit of Ponta Delgada.) Through sheer happenstance my travel companion, Brendan, and I found ourselves in Ponta Delgada for the four days that the festival was taking place.

Throughout the course of the year, a handful of loved ones from home have agreed to join me on my venture. Brendan, who decided he wanted to be a part of my Azores adventure, arrived just two days after I did, and would join me for the next ten days.

"What great luck," Brendan and I said to each other in unison. "What is on the docket for the next couple of days?" we asked the man checking us into our affordable, yet centrally located hotel in Ponta Delgada, which coincidentally happened to be right in the thick of all the craziness surrounding the Divine Holy Spirit festivities.

"*You haven't seen the agenda*?!" the man nearly screamed, puzzled as to how we were possibly staying in the middle of the action without knowing any of the details of the festivities.

The excitement in this man's voice, coupled with the undeniable buzz in the streets, led me to believe that the next four days were going to be action-packed. "Did we just stumble upon the Azorean version of Germany's Oktoberfest?" I asked Brendan, who, in general, is just as clueless as I am. My excitement level shot through the roof.

So you can imagine my disappointment when, moments later, I was presented with the series of events that would be taking place the four days we were in town, and the one word that kept jumping off the page.

Parade.

For as long as I can remember, I have always loathed parades.

It probably has something to do with the fact that my undiagnosed ADD disorder prevents me from sitting still long enough for a red light to turn green, let alone an entire parade to pass me by. But to this day, if you are a parade, and your name isn't the SpectroMagic Nighttime Parade in Disney World's Magic Kingdom, don't even talk to me.

On a related note: RIP SpectroMagic Nighttime Parade, you are a legend. October 1, 1991 - June 4, 2010

My excitement about being in Ponta Delgada for the big festival wore off quicker than it appeared, and now I was just bitter about having to endure three parades, right outside my door, over the next four days.

And I am not just talking about quick little whirlwind parades that last a half an hour and then the roads are clear, and the spectators disappear. I am talking about nearly ALL DAY parades right in front of my damn hotel.

The first day of the festival was parade-free, which enabled me to explore the beautiful town of Ponta Delgada. We went for a long walk along the seawall, visited the old churches and monuments, and explored Fort Saint Blaise, which defended the town against pirate attacks. We even found time to visit the Gruta do Carvao, an underground lava tube, spending about 8 Euro for all the activities combined. Most importantly, we were able to map out our next three days, avoiding the parade route at any and all costs.

On day two we went on a beautiful, yet exhausting 11-kilometer walk to the neighboring town of Lagoa. We were able to escape Ponta Delgada right before the parade congestion started filling the sidewalks, and by the time we returned, the parade was over, the streets were cleared, and there wasn't a balloon, popcorn, or a parade float in sight.

On day three, however, the plan was a bit more difficult to execute. There was a brand new casino just built in Ponta Delgada, so naturally, being quite the gambling man, I wanted to check it out. I figured I would get to the casino around noon, just as the parade was about to begin. I would spend about three hours losing all my allotted money on blackjack and roulette, and by the time my ATM card wouldn't allow me to withdraw any more money for the day, the parade would be over and I would once again have avoided the dreary procession.

There was, however, one caveat.

The parade route started DIRECTLY outside of the new hotel/casino.

No problem. I'll just get my ass out of bed early and get to the casino before the parade starts, I said to myself, still confident that my plan would work and I would soon be spending a beautiful,

19

sunny Azorean afternoon losing all my hard-earned money in a cold, dark casino.

So around 10:30 a.m. Brendan and I emerged from our hotel and were delighted to see that the streets were clear, except for a few "early birds" determined to get the best seats in the house. Or as I like to call them, my antithesis.

You should have seen them with their folding chairs, umbrellas, coolers, cameras and smiles. It was disgusting.

And the closer we got to the casino, the birth canal of the parade, the more early birds were already gathered, ready for an "action-packed" day of sitting, watching, and presumably a whole lot of waving. And whatever the hell else people do at parades.

With the casino in clear view, our footsteps grew bigger and bigger until finally, we were standing at both the entrance of the divine gambling hall, as well as the demonic front lines of the parade.

Without so much as a glance in the direction of the parade, I walked up to the casino doors, enthusiastically tried pushing them open, and promptly walked straight into the glass.

Like the majority of European doors, I never get it right when it comes to opening them. If you are supposed to push open a door, I will pull it, and if you are supposed to pull open a door, I will push it. I swear they decide what feels like the most natural way to open a door, and then they do the opposite.

After laughing off the mishap, and having a few choice words for Brendan, who was uncontrollably laughing, I grabbed the massive casino door handle and pulled. The door didn't budge.

So I pulled harder.

Nothing.

Then I pushed again.

Still nothing.

Feeling the panic start to rise, and the blood starting to rush to my head, I frantically looked around for an explanation as to why the doors were not opening. I was dumbfounded.

So we walked around to the hotel's lobby that was attached to the casino and asked them why the casino doors were locked.

"The casino does not open until 2:00 p.m.," was their nightmare-of-an-answer.

After the shock wore off, and I regained control of all of my senses, I looked at Brendan and said, "Now what the fuck are we going to do?"

I looked to my right, and the sidewalks were jam-packed with spectators that looked bored to tears. I looked to my left and the floats and vehicles, and kids and adults were lining up, preparing for their big parade through town that was to begin in a half hour. I have to admit, however, that the atmosphere in the parade participant's pregaming festivities area did seem pretty lively.

Realizing we were stuck between a rock and a hard place, and weighing both options, I told Brendan that I would rather be a part of the damn parade than suffer through watching it go by.

Then a lightbulb went off in my head.

Why not make our own parade by walking at our own pace in the opposite direction of the stationary parade. Everyone was already in full costume. All the floats were in place. And it did look like they were having a hell of a good time.

So we snuck past the imaginary starting line that separated the parade from the spectators and crossed over into the "parade participants" section.

The beginning of the line-up was akin to what it must have looked like when Noah was loading up his ark and preparing for his journey; there were dozens of animals being led to their starting place. Bulls, cows, horses, goats, and animals that I didn't know existed were ready to entertain the people of Ponta Delgada. But, instead of watching them slowly march by, Brendan and I got to go up to the animals, feed them, pet them, and were even invited to take a quick ride in a horse-drawn carriage.

Knowing that we were in an area we were not supposed to be, we were sure we were going to be asked to leave and head to the spectators section of the parade at any minute.

But that didn't happen. In fact, quite the opposite happened.

Seeing as we were both wearing H&M button-down shirts with palm trees and umbrellas on them, and both wearing baseball caps, and both so very obviously American tourists, the people of Ponta Delgada were just as captivated by us as we were by them.

Instead of getting yelled at for being there, people were calling us over to them. We were offered an abundance of food including breads, cakes, crabs, fish, and most paramount, beers. I suddenly found myself in a section that actually had floats with kegs of beer on them and floats that had woodfire ovens to cook breads and pizzas. It looked exactly as I would imagine it would look like if my hometown threw a parade dedicated to me... one raft of pizza followed by multiple rafts of nothing but kegs of locally brewed beer.

The people in that Ponta Delgada parade treated us like family, and the only thing they wanted in return was to know about our lives and ask us questions about what we were doing in Ponta Delgada and if we were enjoying the festivities.

The dancers put on dance performances just for us. The singers sang their songs for us. The bands played their instruments for us. Just about everyone asked us why we were walking in the opposite direction of the parade. "Aren't you going to stay and watch the parade?" they would ask.

We, of course, lied and told the generous parade people that we had to meet friends in the neighboring town because I did not have the heart to tell them that I am not physically or mentally capable of participating in parade-watching. We thanked them for their generosity and sadly walked to explore the parade-free section of town.

But three important things happened that day.

- I fell in love with the people of Ponta Delgada. Not only for their generosity, but for their passion and dedication to their culture. The amount of pride they showed for their community was something I will never forget.

- The SpectroMagic Nighttime Parade in Disney World's Magic Kingdom became no longer the only parade I have ever enjoyed.

- At 2:00 p.m., filled to the brim with bread, cake, pizza, crabs and Azorean beer, I made a hearty donation to the town and people of Ponta Delgada in the form of blackjack chips at their brand new casino.

3. Azores, Portugal
Luxury Budget
Unsolved Mystery at Spa Resort

For the most part, when traveling, there are four options for accommodation types; hostels, airbnb / guest house rentals, hotels, or resorts. Each accommodation type has benefits that the others may not have.

For this *Venture Twelve* project, the nights I am traveling on a low budget are usually spent at hostels or campgrounds, the nights I am on a moderate budget are usually spent at hotels or an airbnb, and the nights I am traveling on a luxury budget are typically spent at resorts.

By far the biggest benefit of staying at hostels is the fact that you get to meet people from all over the world. In fact, on the *Venture Twelve* trip, I made dozens of friends that I will stay in contact with for years, if not for the rest of our lives. At hostels, people talk to each other, people get to know each other, and socializing is welcomed and encouraged.

The biggest benefit of moderately priced hotels is that you get the most for your money. You have your privacy and comfort, but you do not necessarily have to break the bank.

And, of course, the biggest benefit of resorts is the option of luxury. Most resorts will have fine dining, spas, beautiful swimming pools, bathrobes, slippers, fancy bars, and of course, top notch service.

Most resorts are designed for couples to get away from the hustle and bustle of everyday life and have time for some peace and quiet. Socializing with other resort guests is typically not a priority, and oftentimes avoided at all costs.

But that doesn't mean that everyone isn't aware of who they are sharing their resort paradise with. Let's face it, despite all the options of luxury, lounging around a resort all day can be quite boring, so you have no other option but to people-watch.

At resorts you will usually see the same people at breakfast, lunch, dinner, the pool, the hot tub, the bar or the gym. Friendly nods of acknowledgment or fake smiles are exchanged, and you go about your separate ways.

With all that being said, my travel buddy Brendan and I are not ones to fade into the background. We are both overly friendly, people-people, that tend to be the life of the party.

But at luxurious Azorean resorts, most people find no need for "life of the party" types.

While I had a four-night stay at the beautiful Pedras do Mar Resort & Spa on Sao Miguel island, Brendan had to return home, therefore only had two nights at the resort, which meant I was flying solo for my final two days in the Azores.

The Pedras do Mar Resort & Spa sits perched upon a cliff surrounded by the Atlantic Ocean. If you step out of the infinity pool and walk 46 steps, you will be on the edge of a cliff with one of the most spectacular views you can imagine. If you take 47 steps, you will fall to a horrific death. If you ever need a death to look like an accident, have I got the place for you.

For the two days that Brendan and I stayed at the resort we were impossible to miss. Two American guys that were the first to order pitchers of sangria in the morning, the first two to jump into the infinity pool in the afternoon, the guys hysterically laughing at the fancy restaurant, and the guys cheersing non-stop at the bar.

I can not be positive, but I am pretty sure we were the envy of every guy that was at the resort with his girlfriend or wife, and the cause of many an eye roll from each of their corresponding girlfriends or wives.

But on day three at the luxury resort, Brendan had an early flight back to the States, while I still had two nights in paradise before making my way to mainland Portugal. His flight was an early morning one, meaning he had to get a taxi before sunrise, and by the time breakfast was served, Brendan was on a flight back home, and I was at the resort without my partner in crime.

At breakfast, instead of seeing two Americans drinking a pitcher of sangria like the resort guests were accustomed to, they saw one American, solemnly drinking a cappuccino.

The guests probably chalked Brendan's absence from breakfast up to him sleeping in, or being a bit hungover and choosing to skip breakfast.

At pool time in the afternoon, instead of seeing two Americans competing to see who can swim back and forth underwater more times, risking their lives just to get a few meters farther than the other, they saw me, reading a book while sitting on the ledge of the pool.

"Some hangover that less handsome, and far less charismatic American must be having, we haven't seen him all day," is what I am imagining most of the resort guests were saying to each other at this point.

But it wasn't until dinner that I realized that people were actually beginning to question each other about where Brendan was, and why I was suddenly "vacationing" at a luxury resort all by myself.

"Don't look now, but that American is still by himself," was the topic of most dinner conversations that evening.

"Is the other guy ill?"

"Did they get into an argument?"

After dinner, I retired to my room for an early night. I had a long day planned for the next day that included lounging by the pool for eight hours and pretending like I was going to use the resort gym later.

On the second day after Brendan left, I could tell people were growing more concerned. After all, we are on an island in the middle of the Atlantic Ocean. People don't just go home without their friends. When two people are at a resort on an island, 99.9% of the time they come together and they leave together.

It doesn't help that Brendan left at five in the morning, meaning that none of the resort guests saw him with his luggage, or heard us saying "Goodbye bro," or "Have a safe trip home, buddy," or "Thanks for coming with me, this was a blast, love ya man!"

Instead, they were left letting their imagination run wild.

On my final night at the resort, before dinner, just as the sun was setting, I noticed a light shining down by the cliff.

It turned out to be four hotel guests walking the cliff's edge shining a flashlight down onto the jagged rocks below. This was my fourth day at the resort and all of these people have been there since I arrived, yet I had never seen the two couples speak to each other.

That's nice. Those two boring couples made friends with each other. Now instead of two boring bumps on a log, they can be four moderately less boring bumps on a log, I thought to myself.

They walked up and down the cliff flashing the light and searching for something, as one would do if you lost the back of an earring and made everyone in your vicinity help in your search of finding it.

After about 15 minutes they all returned to the resort, walking right by where I was reading my book and drinking my gin and tonic. I gave each of them my customary fake smile of acknowledgment, but not a single one of them returned the gesture, which struck me as quite odd, not to mention, pretty damn rude.

The two couples sat together that night at dinner for the first time. All chatting way more than they had done previously. They finally found some common bond that they could converse about.

I chose to eat dinner sitting at the resort bar that night, as it seemed much less awkward than sitting at a fine dining establishment alone.

After the couples finished eating, one of the guys came up to the bar, ordered a beer, and sat next to me. He introduced himself as Chris, and offered up the information that he, too, was from the States. I could tell that "Chris from the States" was not sitting next to me and making small talk because he wanted to make a new friend. He was up to something.

"So… may I ask you a question?" Chris asked. "What the hell happened to that guy you were with?"

"Oh, my friend Brendan? He fell off the cliff a few days ago," I said without missing a beat.

It's hard to explain the expression on Chris' face, but it was a combination of both horror and disbelief, with a dash of I-KNEW-IT!

After silently staring at each other for about five seconds, I told him I was kidding and Brendan is back in America, after taking an early morning flight the day before because he had to return to work and I was heading to mainland Portugal the next day.

"Can I ask YOU a question?" I asked Chris.

"Sure," he replied.

"Did you start talking to that other couple because you all were talking about why I was suddenly alone and were making guesses as to where my friend went?"

"Yup," Chris answered, also without missing a beat.

"Dude, we were actually all down by the cliff a few hours ago with a flashlight looking to see if we could see a body," he said, only half-joking. "We were sure you got into a fight and pushed him off the cliff. Based on the way you two argued about who went further underwater in the pool, and which of you drank more of the sangria pitcher, we were sure you were betting on who could get closest to the edge without falling off or something."

"That makes sense, I suppose. We are quite competitive and do fight like an old married couple sometimes," I confessed.

And with that, Chris from the States and I clinked our drinks and he returned back to his table of four. The other three all leaned in as he retold our conversation. I saw the look of horror on the girls' faces as he told them Brendan "Fell off the cliff," then the following laughter that ensued as he told them what actually happened. Simultaneously all three strangers, and Chris, turned and looked at me, grinning from ear to ear. We all air-cheers'd, as I finished my drink and headed back to my room, satisfied that I was the reason these four duds actually started having fun in paradise.

The following morning I woke up wondering how many more people at the resort were thinking the same thing as Chris and his crew.

So before I checked out, I did one last walk through the pool area. This time, however, I was on a fake phone call, talking loud enough for the pool area to hear. I easily could have pretended I was talking to Brendan, and telling him how happy I was that he got home safely, and how much I missed him the past two days. This would reassure all the nosy resort guests that Brendan's corpse was not decaying on the rocks just below the cliff's edge, and ease their worried minds.

Instead, I was pretending to be talking to someone back home saying "I am not sure what happened to him. The last time I saw him was right before I went for a walk by the cliff. When I came back he was gone. His stuff is still in the room. But I am sure he is fine."

Then I calmly walked to reception, gave them my key, and hopped in a taxi to take me to the airport and begin my next venture.

4. Marrakech, Morocco
Low Budget
The Snake Swindler

There are not many places on Earth that are so geographically close, but such extreme polar opposites as Portugal and Morocco. Just a quick drive through the southern tip of Spain, and a short ferry ride separates the two countries, yet you will feel like you have time-traveled through a parallel universe.

The symphony of church bells politely alerting you to the time in Portugal is replaced by the blares of call to prayer that radiate out of all the mosques in the area.

The cool ocean breeze from the coast of Lisbon is replaced by the hot, thick, stifling air looming in the city of Marrakech.

And the friendly, welcoming Portuguese that will invite you into their homes and cook you a homemade dinner wanting nothing in return, are replaced with friendly, welcoming Moroccans, many, certainly not all, with the intention of trying to swindle as much money from you as possible. That is not meant as an insult, or cautionary tale, as much as it is a reflection of their way of making a living. The Moroccan culture thrives on tourism and trying to make as much money out of unsuspecting tourists as possible.

After getting mildly swindled in the port city of Tangier, as well as the Blue City of Chefchaouen, my newest travel partner, Dan, and I made our way to Marrakech, Morocco. Dan was a teacher with me back home and despite being several years older than me[1], he joined me in mainland Portugal after I left the Azores

---

[1] Four

and after taking a very long detour through Spain, France and Andorra, traveled with me to Morocco, where we would part ways.

We promised ourselves that we would not be swindled by any offers of guidance, private tours, or promises of "good deals" to try and persuade us to purchase Moroccan goods that we did not need, nor had the means of transporting back to the United States.

After inadvertently finding ourselves on "tours" we didn't mean to partake in when in "The Blue City" of Chefchaouen, we now (wrongfully) considered ourselves experts in Moroccan culture, and it was time to show off how travel-savvy we were by taking on the streets of Marrakech. Nobody was going to pull a fast one over on us this time. We were on a low budget and therefore couldn't afford to get swindled again.

And boy did we stick to our guns... after checking in to our insanely awesome riad right in the heart of the city, we strolled down the alleyways of Marrakech as confident as any Americans with button-down, bright floral print shirts possibly could.

A riad is a type of traditional Moroccan house or palace with an interior garden or courtyard. They are normally exceptionally cheap and come with a free breakfast of Moroccan tea, fruits, yogurt, croissants, harcha, a round bread with corn-bread like texture, and of course, hard-boiled eggs, which seem to be a staple at all Moroccan breakfasts.

As we journeyed through narrow alleys filled with shops selling everything one could possibly imagine purchasing, we began to explore the beautiful city of Marrakech. We shrugged off all offers of "Join us on the best tour in Marrakech." We non-nonchalantly hollered back "America," as locals questioned "My brothers, where are you from?" And we kept our eyes forward and steady on the prize... the center square of Marrakech; Jemaa el-Fnaa.

As it was Dan's last night on the venture with me, I selflessly said, tell me what you want to do in Marrakech, and we will do it.

He responded immediately with ... "I want to see a snake charmer."

"That seems cheap enough," I said, relieved that he didn't say anything that would fall out of my low budget range. It was settled, we would find a snake charmer, regardless of the fact that we are both scared shitless of snakes.

Just a few moments passed and whether by fate or by the good karma that we have accumulated along the way, the alleyway opened up into a bustling square that can only be referred to as the Times Square of Morocco.

Perhaps even more miraculous, the very first thing we see is a small crowd of people gathered around a snake charmer, his four "helpers," and five terrifying snakes.

From a safe enough distance that if the snakes decided they were hungry, they would eat someone closer to them before us, we snapped a quick picture of one of the cobras, confirmed that the picture was "good enough" and began walking away, preparing to explore this electrifying square.

That is until one of the snake charming assistants yelled to us "My brothers, give me your camera. Where are you from? Let me take a picture of the snakes with you two in the picture."

We both murmured that we are all set, but Moroccan snake charming assistants do not take "No thank you," for an answer, and before we knew it, we were in the midst of a photoshoot with cobras, pythons, and an audience of travelers that were very likely whispering to each other "Look at the American idiots that just got swindled by the snake charmer."

After about three minutes of being the closest human beings to cobras, the snake charmer / swindler gave me back my camera and asked for 400 Dirhams (about $40 USD). We looked at each other, and didn't need to verbally say *We are the dumbest people alive*, because we both already knew what each other was thinking... *We are the dumbest people alive.*

Normally, we probably would have just given the snake charming assistant 400 dirham and chalked it up as paying a few bucks each for once-in-a-lifetime photos, but the problem was we only had about 50 dirham between the two of us, and neither the snake charmer, nor his assistants would even entertain the fact that $5 USD was sufficient for the entire photo shoot.

Like middle school children that were in the principal's office, we talked through the options of getting ourselves out of this mess. "We can delete the pictures," said Dan.

"We can give you 50 dirham now, and I'll come back tomorrow and give you the rest," I offered.

But the snake charmer assistant was not having it. Neither of these options were good enough for him. "I took for you many, many of the BEST pictures you can get. Now I need you to pay me 400 dirhams," the man pleaded.

After pulling the snake charming assistant aside and privately debating back and forth with the man, Dan and the snake charmer came upon a solution. Dan would find the nearest ATM while I was, for lack of a better term, "held hostage."

So I suddenly find myself in the middle of the busiest square in Marrakech, like I was in an imaginary holding cell and the snakes were my watchguards. They were staring at me just as evil as I was staring at them. All while thinking, *if these snakes even give the slightest inclination that they are going to move even a centimeter towards me, I am going to either scream like an infant or simply drop dead right on the spot.*

Every time a new tourist would walk up to the snakes and try to take a picture I would say, underneath my breath, just loud enough for only them to hear, "I wouldn't do that if I were you. They totally screwed us, and now I am being held hostage."

Not knowing whether to laugh or to run and tell the authorities that I was being held captive, most of the tourists smiled, said "Thanks for the advice," and carried on their merry way. Glancing back every now and then to see if I was really being forced to stay there, or if I was just hanging out on the snake charmer's magic carpet just for the hell of it on my own free accord.

After the longest ten minutes in the history of recorded time, Dan returned back with the 400 dirhams, and I was released from the confines of which I was contained. But not before I very sternly made it known to the snake charming assistant, "That wasn't very nice. You tricked us."

"But they are very nice pictures. You look very nice with the snakes," the main snake charming assistant told me, as he was counting the dirhams that Dan gave him in exchange for my freedom.

"Thank you for the compliment," I said calmly to the man, "But the point is that you shouldn't hold people hostage. It is not a nice thing to do."

"Take one more picture with you and me and the snake," said the snake charmer assistant. "You will not have to pay."

So, using poor judgement and throwing caution to the wind, I stood with the man as he wrapped the cobra around my neck and I posed with him for yet another photo shoot. After hugging the man, and telling him I was sorry for being mad at him for being held at the snake carpet against my will, he apologized for holding me captive.

As we were walking away with our cameras, we heard the man yell "PLEASE MAYBE GIVE A LITTLE BIT FOR THOSE LAST PICTURES THAT WE TOOK. THEY ARE VERY NICE PICTURES!"

Dan and I stared at each other and simultaneously said one word…

"RUN!"

Ultimately Dan and I narrowly escaped getting cheated and ripped off by a snake charmer two times within a matter of minutes, and after our escape we once again promised ourselves we will never be swindled by a charismatic, Moroccan salesman ever again.

5. Fez, Morocco
Moderate Budget
The Horrible Hagglers

When it comes to traveling, we all have our strengths. Some people seem to have a built in compass and can navigate themselves around a city after being there for just a few minutes. Some people have a knack for meeting fellow travelers and expanding their social circle for a few hours, a day, a night, or even longer. Some people are so budget savvy that they can get the absolute best deals possible by clipping coupons, finding two-for-one deals, or asking their accommodations to match a deal they found on a particular website.

Ideally, each member of your travel group will have their own unique strengths to compensate for each other's travel weaknesses. Fortunately, a portion of my time in Morocco was spent with Erin, a former teacher turned sommelier and the Bonnie to my Clyde.

We both have individual skills that allow us to *appear* to be travel masters. Erin is great at remembering important streets, directions, recommendations we pick up along the way, and the names of wines that I particularly enjoy. You know, the basics.

While sometimes it can be a huge weakness, my biggest travel strength is that I can become friends with just about anybody. Whether it be a server at a restaurant, a bartender while having some nighttime beverages, a taxi driver, the manager of a hotel, strangers on a trolley, flight attendants, solo travelers, bachelor/bachelorette parties, or wandering Moroccan nomads in the Sahara Desert, if you leave me alone for a few minutes, you will likely find me with a new best friend for the night.

This is an important skill because not only are we meeting new people from all over the world and learning about new cultures from friendly locals, but also because it enables us to not have to talk to each other for a while. This allows for a much needed break when anyone is traveling with just one other person.

Neither of us, however, are without our travel flaws. When it comes to me and Erin, one flaw in particular is evident from even an outsider's perspective. The sad, but true fact of the matter is that we are both absolutely pitiful when it comes to the act of haggling.

This is not much of an issue when traveling in the United States, or major European cities. When traveling on a moderate budget in Fez, Morocco, however, having the skill set to be able to haggle comes in quite handy.

Fez is littered with souks, which are little shops, stands, or in some cases simply blankets on the ground, in which locals sell products ranging from beautiful handmade Moroccan pottery, elaborate Arabian carpets, and the finest leather purses to souks selling only finger nail clippers, or mystery jars of what appears to be a jelly substance...or perhaps their most popular item, a package of tissues.

On a side note: in Fez, locals, usually children, will walk up to you, not say a single word, and hold a package of tissues in your face. Do not panic. You likely do not have gelato on your face, or something hanging from your nose, they are just trying to make a buck, or in this case, whatever you deem the going price should be for about six one-ply tissues.

So on this day in Fez, Erin's first day on the venture, she was anxious to get her shopping on and after walking about 15 steps from our Riad in the middle of the Fez medina, she already had a pair of Moroccan shoes (which were hideous if you want my honest opinion) in her hand. I approached just in time to hear her pathetic haggling skills in action.

When Erin questioned the shoe seller "How much?" he responded with 180 dirhams (About $18 USD). Trying her best to look like she knew how to haggle, Erin responded as if she was insulted at the offer, and said something along the lines of "NO WAY! How about 100 dirhams?"

The Moroccan shoe maker apparently saw right through her bull and immediately called her bluff, saying, "Oh no, this is good quality, very good quality. 180 dirhams."

World traveler Erin's response was, "OK. They are nice," and handed the man the 180 dirham with not so much as a "How about 150?"

After all the shoe-buying excitement, and after lecturing Erin that we are on a moderate budget, not luxury, for four days and shouldn't be buying Moroccan crap that we don't need, we decided to get some sightseeing under our belts. We opted for a palace that seemed within walking distance, but due to the fact that it was hotter than the seventh layer of hell, we really wanted to get out of the sun.

"Should we walk, or get a taxi?" I asked while trying our best to not pull out a map, due to the fact that maps in Morocco basically have the force of the Earth's magnetic plate, attracting any and every Moroccan in sight so they can "help us." And by "help us," I mean "get a tip."

So we make the irrational decision to hop in a taxi without first asking the taxi driver how much it would be or how far away the palace was. This is basically the first thing they tell you exactly not to do on the first day of Travel 101 class. Especially when you are supposed to be careful about your budget.

We asked the taxi driver to take us to the palace and less than two minutes later, we were dropped off directly in front of our accommodation. We walked across the street to the palace that we had no idea was our neighbor. It cost about $9 USD for a ride that was quicker than Space Mountain at Disney World. Chalk up another loss for Ryan and Erin.

After an uneventful trip to the palace, and getting cheated out of $9 USD from our very unsympathetic taxi driver, Erin already needed to get to an ATM.

As I waited for her with my back to Erin and the ATM while taking in the scenery of the main square at the Fez medina, I was approached by a man selling authentic Moroccan shirts. He taps me square on the chest, and says, in broken English, "You will look good in Moroccan shirt. It is good quality."

I brush off the man, and say "No, No, No, I am just waiting for her (pointing to Erin) at the ATM. I will not buy anything."

He insisted that I at least look at all the shirts he has available, and as he flipped through all of them, my eyes kept getting stuck on an amazing royal blue Moroccan shirt with a pattern that even the Egyptian Pharaohs would be jealous of.

But I stayed strong and continued to say "No thank you, my friend, I will not buy anything."

But he, like just about everyone else in Morocco, had a hard time taking "No," "No thank you," "Thank you so much, but I am not interested," and "I am so sorry, but I do not want to buy anything," for an answer. So he continued to stand next to me and tell me how good I would look in the blue shirt that he could tell I was interested in.

Due to my deplorable self-control issues, eventually I made the mistake of saying, "How much?"

"200 dirhams," said the shirt seller.

"No way. 100 is the absolute most I will pay," I said, and began walking back towards the ATM and Erin, who apparently is having a hell of a hard time figuring out how to get her money out.

"OK, my friend, how about this... 150 dirhams, and the shirt is yours. You will look so good".

He is right, that shirt will really bring out my eyes, I thought to myself.

"Deal," I said, pulling out a 200 dirham and handing it to the man.

Feeling proud of myself for actually haggling and saving 50 dirham (about $5 USD) for a killer Moroccan shirt, I watched as the man fumbled through his pockets trying to count the change.

A fun fact about me, however, is that I am physically incapable of holding on to change, as every single time I sit down anywhere, a chorus of clinging and clanging echos from under my seat, and I see the dirhams, euros, or quarters roll in every which direction.

"You know what," I say to the man, just as he finished counting out 50 dirham in coins to hand me.

"Just keep it. It's fine, I lose change. I would rather you have the extra 50 dirham and actually use it, rather than me take it and drop it 30 seconds after I walk away."

And just like that, I once again ended up paying full price for something that I didn't even need.

The Moroccan man and I hugged, and he again told me how very good I am going to look in the royal blue Moroccan shirt.

"Thank you, my friend. I will wear it all around the world," I said, lying more to myself than to the man. "Best of luck selling more shirts," I yelled behind us as we made our way back to the riad with our shoes, shirt, and horrendous haggling skills in tow.

6. Morocco (Sahara)
High Budget
Desert Decadence

In ancient times, long before the advances in astronomical technology we are familiar with today, people would think that a solar eclipse was a sign that the world was ending.

Back in the 7th Century BC a solar eclipse passed over the Greek island of Paros. After the eclipse was over the poet Archilocus wrote…

"Nothing in the world can surprise me now. For Zeus, the father of the Olympian, has turned midday into black night by shielding light from the blossoming Sun, and now dark terror hangs over mankind. Anything may happen."

In 1504 when Christopher Columbus and his crew were nearly starved to death after becoming shipwrecked off the coast of Jamaica, the explorer used a lunar eclipse as a bargaining method with the Arawak Indians, convincing them that he controlled the sky, thus prompting them to provide him and his crew with food, which they obliged.

And back in the 16th century, the proverbial shit hit the fan in the Aztec Empire when a solar eclipse unexpectedly rolled into town. Among the shell-shocked was Franciscan Friar, Bernardino de Sahagun, who is now widely considered to be one of the very first anthropologists. His account of the Black-Friday-like (pun intended) chaos is as follows...

"The Sun turned red, it became restless and troubled. It faltered. Then there were a tumult and a disorder. All were disquieted, unnerved, frightened. There was weeping. The common folk raised a cry, lifting their voices, shrieking. There were shouting everywhere. People of light complexion were slain as sacrifices. Captives were killed. All offered their blood. In all the temples, there was singing and chants. An uproar, there were war cries. It was thus said, if this is complete, it will be dark forever. The demons of darkness will come down, and they will eat men."

Talk about things escalating quickly. The Aztec Empire went from a normal sunny afternoon, presumably filled with hunting, gathering, and carving graffiti into caves (or whatever the hell else they did for fun) into war cries, everybody offering their own blood, and thinking the demons of darkness will come down and eat them, all because of a few seconds of darkness that we now refer to as a solar eclipse.

* *

In present day, the Sahara Desert is the largest hot desert on Earth. It is also one of the driest regions in the world. On average, the month of August in the Sahara Desert contains 30.5 days that are completely bone dry, not even producing a millimeter of precipitation. The other .5 days usually sees anywhere between a whopping 1-3 mm of precipitation, which is basically equivalent to the amount of saliva that comes out of a toddler's uncovered mouth when they sneeze.

So naturally, when we were in Erg Chebbi, the gateway to the Sahara, we had the concerns that any Westerner would have about spending three nights in a tent in the middle of the bone dry desert.

After traveling by van, bus, and taxi to the outskirts of the desert from Marrakech, we were greeted with a private 4x4 which would take us off-roading through the desert dunes and ultimately lead us to our luxury camp to begin our desert experience.

After a few minutes of traversing up, over and around massive sand dunes, one could look in any direction, and see nothing but orange sand surrounding you. Although the Moroccan berber that was driving us seemed confident that we would somehow stumble upon a luxury camp in the middle of all of the massive dunes, it is impossible to not think about all of the worst case scenarios that could happen to you.

What if the 4x4 breaks down?

What if the driver suddenly drops dead and leaves us to fend for ourselves?

What if I spontaneously combust in the back of this 4x4 because of the 120 degree August Moroccan desert sun?

I quickly realize that the third option would be the best case scenario, because if I am going to die in the middle of the desert, it might as well be spontaneously, right?

But miraculously, out of nowhere, we saw eleven white tents in the middle of the bright orange sand dunes. The closer we got, the less panicked we became, until ultimately our 4x4 arrived at our camp, and we were greeted by a dozen berbers covered from head to toe in traditional berber shrouds. All were more eager than the other to help us with our belongings, guide us to the welcoming area, provide us with cool face cloths to help bring our body temperatures out of ICU admission stage, and most importantly, supply us with delicious ice cold alcoholic refreshments.

After a beautiful, yet harrowing journey, we finally made it to our luxury desert camp, and were ready for four days of Moroccan pampering. Our warm welcoming ended with the berbers bringing our luggage to our luxury tent and walking us through our quarters, pointing out the things one would not expect to find in any tent, let alone a tent in the middle of the desert.

Two queen beds, electricity, air conditioning, a working toilet, and a functioning shower, were among the highlights of our glamping experience. After the brief tour, the berbers were not even done zipping up the tent and I already had the air conditioner on full blast and wondering to myself what the appropriate amount of time was before I headed back to the main tent and ordered myself an ice cold Casablanca beer or six.

As the tent began cooling down to my preferred artic-like sleeping conditions, I unpacked my luggage, grabbed my journal, and headed to our backyard; an enormous orange sand dune, which now that I was standing at the foot of, seemed like a massive undertaking to climb, but I attempted it anyway. Plus, this would kill at least a half hour, so when I did end up asking the berbers for beer they wouldn't think I was a complete drunk.

About 20 seconds into my climb I had a sudden newfound respect for camels and the way they ascend the dunes with ease. I instantly regretted eating that delicious camel burger the night before in Fez, and vowed I would never indulge in the delicacy again.

Miraculously I made it to the top of the towering dune, snapped a dozen or so photos of my temporary home below, and opened my journal to write about my journey so far in Morocco. Before I completed even one sentence I realized it was way too hot to be baking in the Sahara Desert sun and found myself gathering up my belongings to head back to the camp below.

But one thing you don't realize until you try it, is that it is extremely difficult to casually walk down a massive desert sand dune. Without meaning to, that walk slowly turns into a jog, which then becomes a run, and before you know it you are in a full sprint running down the orange mountain, inadvertently kicking sand into your own face every step of the way.

And like an out of control skier trying to frantically regain control, you realize the inevitable is going to happen… you are going to fall. And the longer you prolong the fall, the more momentum you will have, and the harder the fall will be. So I let gravity take its course and allowed my body to face-plant into the scorching sand, my belongings being scattered in every which direction, seeing as I lost the ability to hold onto them as my extremities were flailing in the wind.

Upon pulling my face out of the sand I assessed my body for any serious injuries, unable to find any. I quickly began to gather my belongings stunned at how sudden things went wrong, much like the way Jackie Kennedy Onassis began recklessly gathering pieces of her husband's cranium all over the back of the car, while still in shock of the events that just transpired moments before.

I scooted down the dune on my ass the rest of the way and when I reached the bottom, stood up and looked around to make sure nobody saw my disastrous past two minutes. I consider myself to be quite non-violent in general, but at that moment I was convinced that if there were any witnesses I would have no choice but to murder them in their sleep that very night.

Thankfully nobody was in sight, and I limped back into the tent to tell Erin how beautiful the sight was from the top of the sand dune, not mentioning a single word about the face plant.

But after taking one glance at me she burst out laughing.

Shit. She saw me fall. I am never going to hear the end of this for the rest of my life, I thought to myself.

"What the hell happened to you?" she asked.

Relieved that she didn't see my near death experience, I became confused as to how she knew anything even happened to me. Until I heard her say, between fits of laughter, "Look in the mirror."

I glanced to my right where a full-length mirror stood, and saw, what I can only describe as a picture of myself with an Oompa Loompa Snapchat filter covering me from head to toe. I was orange. My hair was orange, my face was orange, my clothes were orange, there was orange sand under my fingernails and globs of orange sand coming out of my ears.

I reluctantly told Erin the story and as she went into an uncontrollable burst of hysterics, I made the decision in my head to not perform CPR on her once she inevitably died of hyperventilation.

After showering off the orange layer and feeling refreshed, I shook off the embarrassment, and confidently walked to the main tent to ask my berber buddies for some well-deserved, ice cold Casablanca beer.

They told me to go back to my tent and they would deliver me my request immediately. Trying to avoid Erin at all costs, who was probably still tweeting about my unfortunate incident, I sat outside our tent and took my chances at sun poisoning rather than look at her and the permanent smile she could not wipe from her face.

As promised, moments later, a bucket of ice cold Casablanca beers arrived at my tent. I tried to chat it up with Said, the berber beer delivery boy, but he said "I am sorry, Sir Ryan, but I must hurry back to the main tent and start preparing for the storm?"

Clearly there was still sand clogging my listening tubes (I am sure there is a scientific term for them, but I am useless when it comes to anything related to Science, so "listening tubes" is the phrase I will be using.)

A storm? But we are in the middle of the fucking desert, I said more to myself than to the young berber that looked at me as if I was an alien that just arrived on the planet.

"Yes sir, look behind you. It is very bad. It has not stormed like this in over eight years. It will be very bad, that is for certain," said the boy that I could tell was beginning to feel sorry for how naive I was.

When I looked behind me at the sky just above where I almost died about 30 minutes prior, I saw the blackest sky I have ever seen in my life. A black hole in the sky was moving towards us at a rapid pace. It was the equivalent of a thousand solar eclipses. An eclipse that was going to last a hell of a lot longer than 96 seconds, or however long eclipses last.

After snapping myself out of a stage of flabbergast, I looked around to the other luxury campers, and if I was filming them, I am positive that they would be casted as extras during the next blockbuster film that portrays the events that transpired during those solar eclipses thousands of years ago.

People were running, screaming, and taking cover. There was tumult. I was half expecting to be slain as a sacrificial ritual.

Oh great, I said to myself. *Now I am going to be locked up in a tent with Erin all night and all I am going to hear about is how I am an Oompa Loompa that fell down the hill.*

… And also, I might die from a hurricane in the middle of the desert.

I gingerly finished the remainder of my beer and walked to the main tent to return the empty bucket.

The berbers, who are complete studs that live in the middle of the desert and can handle anything that comes their way, seemed frazzled and almost a bit panicked about what was approaching.

I yelled "I'll just leave this bucket right here," as if they gave a shit about where my beer bucket was when we were just minutes away from full blown Armageddon.

I began the walk back to the tent and all I could think about was Erin's smiling face, euphoric that she (who tends to be the much more clumsy one between us) could bask in the glory of not being the one that face-planted.

Stopping dead in my tracks, I turned around and headed back to the main tent to find one of the berbers.

"Yes, my friend?" one of them said, as he was carrying approximately 200 pounds of carpet, balanced on what looked to be a very, very heavy chair.

"I hate to bother you, as I know you are preparing for the end of the world and all," I said, calmly, "But do you think I could grab a bottle of wine, seeing as we are going to be locked in the tent. It would be great to ride out the storm with some wine."

"Of course, I will be right back with one," said the boy who could not have been more than 17 years old, and who very likely has never seen any weather phenomenon like this in his entire life.

While he was still in sight, I thought of what an enormous mistake I am making. What the hell am I thinking? A bottle of wine? Locked in a tent? With Erin, who could easily throw back a bottle of wine at Sunday brunch?

"TWO BOTTLES PLEASE!" I yelled, trying to sound urgent, but not demanding.

"Ok, you want two sir?" said the berber, who was probably thinking to himself that this would be the final words he ever uttered… catering to two American wine snobs.

I stared at him like a deer in headlights, and finally after a few seconds of thinking said "Yes, two, thank you so much!"

He had not even turned his back before I yelled "FINE THREE. THAT IS MY FINAL ANSWER!" and laughed at my own joke, as if this kid had ever even heard of *Who Wants to be a Millionaire* let alone knew the catchphrase.

"Ok sir, I will bring you three to your tent. You go now and get in your tent before the lightning comes."

As if on cue, I zipped up my tent and the sky opened up. The wind began blowing the tent from side to side. The thunder was roaring louder than a freight engine. It was as if the beautiful Sahara Desert transformed into literal hell on Earth.

I completely forgot about the wine because I was busy drafting my final words, and was startled when I heard pounding on the tent door.

Erin stared at me, just as frightened.

"You open it," I said.

"No you open it," she replied.

That went on for a solid minute before I got up and unzipped the tent door. Standing there, in the complete dark, his Moroccan headpiece blown half off his head and his shrouds drenched from head to toe, was the young berber. The only way I could tell it was him is when the bolts of lightning would light up the sky just long enough to catch a glimpse of this terrified glare.

"Here is your wine, Sir. Ryan," said the boy. "I will go now if you do not need anything else."

"BE SO SAFE. IT IS REALLY BAD OUT THERE!" I yelled as he disappeared into the darkness.

I could not help but wonder that night, as I lay there, a bottle and a half of wine deep, if the people in ancient times would say "screw it," and drink as much wine as they could when they thought their days were numbered. I sure hope they did.

The next day, after we awoke and realized that we were somehow still alive, we went on a desert excursion to find the wandering nomads of the Sahara Desert. When we approached their "home," they were still dancing. We came to find out that they were just days away from having to pack up all their belongings and find a new place to call home, due to lack of water.

They were so excited about the rainfall that they were laughing, crying tears of joy, and praising God that the rain came and they could stay in their location. They greeted us as if we were heroes that "brought the rain," hugging us, inviting us into their tents, and welcomed us to come back every year.

I may have come close to being responsible for a young Moroccan berber losing his life while delivering me three bottles of wine to my luxury tent during a weather phenomenon, but according to the wandering nomads in the Sahara Desert I was basically royalty.

And who am I to disagree with wandering nomads.

7. Albania, Low Budget
The Hills Are Alive With the Sound of Fighting

Anyone that has ever seen Julie Andrews dancing merrily through the fields, flailing her arms around her body while spinning deliriously about in circles in 1965's *The Sound of Music* can recall the backdrop for where the scene took place.

The lush green fields and enormous snow-topped mountain ranges of Salzburg, Austria, were likely added to the tippity top of many people's "bucket lists," or destinations they would love to visit in their lifetime.

While I didn't manage to make it all the way up to Austria on this venture, I was fortunate enough to spend my low budget days in Theth, Albania, which is a spitting image of where the Von Trapp story was told.

Most Americans think of Albania and the first thing that comes to mind is the violence that once took place there. Never in my wildest dreams did I ever imagine Albania to be towards the very top of my list as far as what I consider to be the most beautiful country in the world. But it unequivocally is.

I swear that Theth, Albania could operate a tour company claiming to be the exact location that Andrews was singing her days away in joyful bliss, and if it weren't for Wikipedia to say otherwise, people would be none the wiser.

Before you finish the rest of this chapter, I implore you to Google search Theth, Albania, just so you know I am not exaggerating.

Not only is Theth breathtakingly gorgeous and an image that will stay with you for the rest of your life, but it is also dirt cheap… if you can survive the harrowing journey there of course.

Unless you are Evel Knievel, or an heir of his, I would highly suggest you do not attempt to drive to Theth yourself, as it is set high in the peaks of the Shala Mountain Range, and requires a tremendous amount of courage to be a passenger, let alone a driver.

So my travel companion, Erin and I, hired a van with a professional driver to take us to our home for the next four days. We stayed in a small, family-owned stone house that I could only describe as something you would see in a fairy tale.

Aside from another family staying at the house, and the family that operated the "bed and breakfast," there was essentially nobody else in sight, save for a few hikers that were passing by and some travelers from a nearby, similar family-owned establishment.

The place was run by an adorable little old Albanian woman. She was about five foot tall, always wore a long, plain dress that went down to her ankles, and wore her hair in a bonnet. Picture Mother Teresa. We were basically staying at Mother Teresa's house if she hadn't donated it to the poor, which I imagine is what she did.

Helping her run the joint was her sister that looked exactly like her, except had a five o'clock shadow and her husband, who only had about two inches on her. She also had the help of her adult children, a woman in her mid-thirties and her husband, and her son about thirty, who basically did all of the manual labor (i.e. mowing the fields, chopping down trees, gathering goats, scaling mountains, or whatever the hell else they need to do to survive up there.)

But the star of the show, hands down, went to her grandson. At eight years of age, he was the host, the server, the expeditor, the sommelier, and basically kept the whole shit-show together.

With the exception of my perfect nephews Andrew and Liam, he was the cutest kid I have ever seen in my life.

Then there was his little sister, who was, and I can not stress this enough, a hellraiser. And that is putting it mildly.

But for $8 USD a night, this place was unbeatable. I could have lived for an entire year up there and spent less than I do on an impromptu trip to TJ Maxx to purchase socks.

They cooked us all of our meals, and supplied us with all the Albanian beer and wine we could drink.

In four days we spent exactly zero dollars on entertainment for the simple reason that there is literally nothing to do up there except take in the beauty. Sure, you can also hike, but hiking is so exhausting and after our one "quick little hike" to the waterfall that the family insisted on us doing that took us seven hours because A) we got lost and B) Erin was wearing FLIP FLOPS(!), we decided to play it safe and spend the rest of our time there reading, writing, and enjoying our surroundings.

It was the definition of complete and utter bliss.

With one exception.

The family HATED each other.

Well, I can not confirm that they actually hated each other, but while they were all lovely people and a delight to be around, (with the exception of the three year old girl who I am convinced was the devil,) all they did was fight with each other.

But who can blame them?

Imagine being secluded from the rest of the outside world, basically stuck in a fairy tale that you can't get out of, with just your immediate family?

They lived together, worked together, spent their free time together, and with the exception of a few occasional guests that didn't speak their language, had nobody else to talk to.

It was basically a form of torture.

We understood the fighting, and felt horrible that we may be the reason they were fighting.

Was someone supposed to give us three eggs instead of two? Did somebody pour our wine glasses too high at dinner, thus prompting the family feud? Did the daughter not properly turn down our beds while we were drinking all of their homemade wine?

We had no idea, because they were fighting in Albanian.

Unless you have ever heard an Albanian family scream at each other upstairs while you were trying not to listen, but also trying very hard to listen at the same time, it may be difficult to imagine the scene that took place those four days.

And to make matters worse, we are situated at the bottom of a valley with a mountain range surrounding us.

Remember the Brady Bunch episode when Bobby and Cindy followed the little Indian boy through the Grand Canyon and got lost and every time the family screamed one of their names the canyon echoed back to them?

That is what the fighting Albanian family sounded like every time we ate breakfast, lunch, or dinner. Or every time we were outside reading a book, or playing cards.

They would scream at the top of their lungs at each other, then the mountains would echo back their screams. Moments later one would arrive with a big smile on their face, asking "është gjithçka në rregull?" meaning "Is everything OK?"

I would smile and say "Shume mire," meaning "Very good," and Erin would smile and say "Me shume vere te lutem," or "More wine please," and they would nod their head and disappear.

Then seconds later, they would pick right up where they left off and start screaming at their loved one again. Or someone new. Who the hell knows?

Maybe Andrews was on to something in Salzburg, Austria. Maybe if the hills of Theth were alive with some music, it would drown out the sound of them being very much alive with the sound of an Albanian family fighting.

...Or maybe the remote hills of Salzburg, Austria were also alive with the sound of quarreling families, but Julie Andrews was too busy "do-re-me-fa-so-la-ti-do'ing" to hear it.

8. Albania – Moderate Budget
Anyone Want to go to Montenegro?

The Balkans are the New England of Europe. Though parts of Greece and Turkey could be considered Balkan territory, it is mainly classified as the ten countries of Albania, Bosnia & Herzegovina, Bulgaria, Croatia, Kosovo, Montenegro, Macedonia, Romania, Serbia, and Slovenia.

While they all share similar histories and climates, there are many defining characteristics to each of the countries that make them stand out from the rest.

For example, some are landlocked while others fall on the coasts of the Adriatic and Black Seas. And surprisingly enough, some are even part of the European Union, while others are not.

But one thing they all share is their undeniable beauty.

For that reason alone, and coupled with the fact that both Erin and I want to visit as many countries as possible in our lifetimes, when we were in Albania we constantly found ourselves talking about how close we were to other countries, and what a shame it would be to not check as many off our lists as possible during our time in the Balkans.

After leaving the fairy tale land of Theth, Albania, we returned to the town of Shkoder, where we had our modest accommodations and would stay for a few days until it was time for Albanian luxury in Durres.

Shkoder is a beautiful little town on the edge of Lake Skadar, with stunning mountain top views, and a quaint, yet modern outdoor shopping plaza filled with trendy restaurants and top-of-the-line shopping options.

We had spent a night in Shkoder before our time in Theth and basically considered ourselves locals when we returned to the town, and to civilization.

We quickly found ourselves back at the plaza, debating what to do with our extra few days in Shkoder, but our conversations always kept returning to the topic of visiting other Balkan countries.

As we were eating a late lunch in the plaza, watching what seemed to be a string of both female and male supermodels walk by (there was a stretch of five minutes where every person that walked by us was more beautiful than the next,) we abruptly came to the decision that we would enjoy our time in Shkoder and stop talking about "other countries," particularly Montenegro which we were closest to. Known for its fortified towns, narrow beaches, and medieval villages, the country was just a few hours away by car. We determined that we would simply just have to come back to the Balkans another time and visit the countries we were unable to explore on this trip.

The plan was set. We would stay in Albania.

We paid our bill and Erin did a healthy amount of boutique shopping (as she does not have to stick to the specific budget level requirements quite the way that I do) before it was time to check into our hotel, which was across a walking bridge. It was about a 15-minute walk from the outdoor plaza we were spending our afternoon to our hotel, and we excitedly began our stroll, knowing that, at just $15 USD a night, our beautiful hotel on the lake would be waiting for us. We would waste the night away in the hot tub under the Albanian stars.

We were content.

As we approached the bridge, we noticed a man standing on the corner with a sign. His back was to us so we could not read the sign, but when he turned around and saw us approaching he yelled to us something inaudible (and in Albanian), so even if it was audible, we still would not have been able to understand.

When we didn't respond, he yelled again, this time in English…

"DOES ANYBODY WANT TO GO TO MONTENEGRO?" this time clear as day.

We both turned around to see who the "anybody" was that the man was referring to, only to find nobody else in sight.

"Did you say Montenegro?" I asked the man.

"Yes, Montenegro," he replied.

"How do we get there?" Erin asked, perplexed as the man was all alone, with no car or any other mode of transportation.

"A bus, it will be here soon," the tall, clean-cut Albanian man said.

Without even looking at each other, or knowing where the hell in Montenegro we were going, we both simultaneously yelled "SURE!"

It was, afterall, this adventurous spirit that we both share that had led us to where we were anyway.

Then, as quickly as I agreed to the voyage, I remembered that I was only supposed to be traveling on a moderate budget at the time.

"How much?" I asked.

Five dollars, roundtrip, the man said.

"How about four dollars" I said, "Five dollars is a bit steep."

The man did not realize I was 100% joking and gladly would have paid the extra dollar, but a huge smile came across his face, as he said "You have got a deal."

Within minutes a large bus came around the corner and started to approach the bridge. The man flagged down the bus as the driver pulled over, opened the door, and said "Montenegro?"

"Yes, two for Montenegro," the man yelled to the driver, as he grabbed our luggage and loaded it onto the bottom of the bus.

"Enjoy your trip, my friends," he hollered to us, as we boarded the bus and sat down in the only two remaining seats, directly behind the driver.

We waved to him through our window and he waved back, the way that parents wave to their children as they depart for their first day of Kindergarten.

The bus was eerily silent despite being filled to capacity, almost as if there was a rule where you were not allowed to speak or you would not be allowed entrance into Montenegro. Some people were fast asleep as if they were on the commute home after the hardest working day of their lives. A few were glaring out the window, watching the mountains come and go, only a handful with headphones in their ears.

But a shocking number of passengers were simply staring straight ahead. They were doing nothing at all except staring straight at the front of the bus, as if they themselves, were in charge of the navigation.

And just like that, Erin and I were heading to the country of Montenegro on a whim, with a busload of boring, book-less librarians.

"How do we get back to Shkoder?" we whispered to each other.

"Sorry to bother you, but where exactly in Montenegro is this bus taking us?" we whispered to the person next to us, who spoke no English, and already seemed annoyed with us.

"I hope there is a hotel available for us to sleep where we are going," we nervously said under our breaths.

But we would have to cross that bridge when we got to it, as we were without Wi-Fi for the duration of our journey. For now, all we could do was sit back, relax, and take in the scenery as we headed to our next Balkan country.

That is, of course, if I had the ability to sit back and relax like a normal human being. Sadly, I don't.

Before we were even out of Shkoder, I was pestering Erin with questions like...

"Should we draft our teams to gamble on the new season of *Survivor*?"

"Let's each rank our top 20 favorite concerts we have ever been to."

"Do you want to see who can guess the exact time we will arrive at the border of Montenegro, and the person who comes closest will get dinner bought by the loser?"

"Let's play cards, OK?"

There was no use in trying to whisper anymore, seeing as everytime we tried to whisper to one another as if we were not allowed to talk, we realized how silly we were and would start laughing uncontrollably; loud enough for the whole bus to hear.

We would play cards, but seeing as we are both ultra-competitive, each game would end up in a dispute or heated disagreement, disrupting the entire bus out of their trances.

After about two and a half hours we approached the Montenegro border (For posterity: I won the bet and as a result, later that night Erin was required to pay for a lovely candlelit dinner on the beach.)

By now, the entire bus all knew the loud Americans, as well as our favorite American Idol winners of all time, our favorite historical figures of all time, and our favorite letters of the alphabet of all time, just to name a few. I am willing to bet that they were all itching for us to get far, far away from them.

As is customary with many busses that cross borders, a border patrol agent will come onto the bus while the bus is waiting in line, and check passports.

Seeing as we were sitting in the front seats, we were the first stop on the border patrol agent's route.

"Passports," the Albanian border patrol agent coldly said to us, dressed in a soldier's uniform, complete with firearms.

Without hesitation, Erin whipped hers out of her carry on and handed it to the man, as he inspected it, starred at Erin, then back at the passport, and then back at Erin before handing it back over to her.

"You?" he said to me, as I was frantically searching my pockets.

"Sorry, one second please," I said, as I began searching through my carry on.

I wasn't looking, but I could physically feel the eyes of the soldier, as well as the eyes of the entire bus raging with fire through my soul.

"Would you mind just quickly doing the rest of the bus first?" I asked, as he continued to stare at me, and I continued to frantically empty out my bag looking for my passport.

He took one glance at the rest of the bus and said "They are not a problem. I need yours."

Sweat was now pouring down my face as I looked at Erin and said "Do you have it?"

"Why would I have it?" she rebutted.

She was right, there was no way I could pin this blame on her.

"Is it in your luggage underneath the bus?" she suggested.

Fuccccccck, I said to myself. And probably out loud too, for good measure.

"My passport is under the bus," I confessed to the soldier, the way a guilty child would confess to his teacher when he tells them that he didn't do his homework.

The soldier then said something in Albanian to the driver which made him turn around, stare at me like I was a complete moron, and shake his head disapprovingly. He then forcefully turned the gigantic steering wheel of the bus, forcing us all out of the customs line and pulled aside so the stupid American could get out of the bus and dig through his luggage for a passport that may or may not be in there.

Luckily for me, I was on a bus full of mute people that sat in complete silence for a *bare minimum* of two and a half hours, because if I was on any other bus IN THE ENTIRE WORLD, I would have descended the steps of the bus to the roar of "BOOOOO" and "YOU SUCK" that all ten Balkan countries would be able to hear simultaneously.

Pro Travel Tip: If a strange man ever stops and asks you if you want to get on a bus and head to a new country, do yourself a favor and make sure you have your passport on your body.

You can thank me later.

9. Albania - Luxury Budget Albanian Jackpot

Back in 2010 a team of Australian-German scientists at Freie University and the Queensland Institute conducted a series of experiments to determine the attention span of the species known as Drosophila Melanogaster, commonly referred to us non-scientists idiots simply as a fruit fly.

Their findings were way too complicated for me to even partially understand, but in summary, this is what I gathered…

Fruit flies have horrific attention spans.

Back in the mid-late eighties and throughout the nineties, it didn't take a team of Australian-German scientists, but instead a group of annoyed teachers, to inform my parents four times a school year, that their son, Ryan, has a horrific attention span.

And all throughout my life, it wasn't my inability to pay attention to things that drove my brother crazy, it was my complete and utter lack of patience.

"You have the patience of a wild boar," is the phrase he would so often use each time he observed me having to wait for something… anything.

Even today I refuse to wait in line at Dunkin' Donuts if there are more than two cars. I have also, multiple times, refused to make important deposits at the bank because I could clearly see there were no available tellers to immediately satisfy my needs. And don't even get me started about lines at Disney World. If I don't have a FastPass for an attraction, my ass will not be riding it, no matter where it falls on my list of the "Top 10 Greatest Disney Attractions of All Time."

Another, let's say "quirk" of mine, to put it lightly, is that while I may not have full blown OCD, seeing as I am never on time for anything, my outfits rarely match, and I have absolutely no fear of being contaminated by germs whatsoever, it is certainly fair to say that I have some extreme neurotic compulsions.

For example, ever since I was a child I would play a game with myself anytime I walked to the mailbox. I would count, sometimes in my head, sometimes out loud, as I attempted to take EXACTLY 25 steps to retrieve the mail, and then exactly 25 steps back to the house.

My Aunt Joy lives two houses down from me, and everytime I go to her house, I make sure I get there in exactly 100 steps, sometimes even having to take a few quick little baby steps, or giant leaps at the end should my estimating be off. If my cousins Renee' or Mark happen to be outside and start talking to me, I simply put my finger up, signaling to them that they will have to wait until I touch their door until I can even begin to think about speaking to them.

So to summarize, in general, I have the attention span of a fruit fly, the patience of a wild boar, and the neurotic tendencies of… whatever animal has the most neurotic tendencies, I have too much ADD to do the research at the moment.

Luckily, I also tend to be as laid back as a koala, and have the social skills and friendly nature of a dolphin.

It all evens out in the wash. I think anyway.

So when Erin and I walked into our suite at the top of the Adriatik Hotel in Durres, Albania to begin our stay in luxury, I walked exactly twenty steps to the large, quadruple set of windows, slid open the expensive, blue curtains (because it has to be the very first thing I do when I step into any hotel room for the first time) and breathed in the view of the Adriatic Sea.

Below us were fine dining restaurants, beach bars, private cabanas, and of course, the long stretch of beach which went as far as the eye could see in both directions.

But looking out into the sea, something caught my eye. It looked like hundreds of tiny little dots were scattered throughout the sea, almost as if they were groups of buoys randomly placed around, hoping to catch tonight's dinner, which would presumably be prepared by a world class chef.

Upon further inspection, or possibly at Erin's insistence, the details elude me right now, we determined they were not buoys, but indeed, swimmers.

I grew up in Westerly, Rhode Island, known for its beautiful beaches and proximity to the ocean. I myself, was a lifeguard on the beach for five years, and a bartender on the beach for twice as long.

I have never seen human beings that far out in any body of water, so my curiosity peaked.

I immediately threw on my bathing suit, and got down to the beach as quick as I could.

I dropped my towel off at a cabana, and darted to the edge of the sea, stopping just as my feet felt the warmth of the crystal clear aqua waters.

Then I began my task. I took a step into the sea.

One, I said in my head.

I took another step.

Two, I counted.

This went on and on, each time my foot hit the floor of the sea I would count, stopping to turn around at every "100" I reached and quietly celebrated my own personal new record best for how many steps I had walked in a body of water before I was swimming.

200… 300… 400…

Still, I could easily look down and see my abs[2] resting above the water.

At about 500 steps I began to be surrounded by the people I had just seen from my hotel window just minutes prior. I was finally able to put faces to what I thought were large plastic balls tied to a fish-collecting cage when I first looked out into the sea.

Because of those dolphin-like social skills of mine, I couldn't help myself from chatting it up with my daring sea-standing friends.

"Where are you from?" I had to ask anyone within earshot.

"How long are you staying here?" I would follow it up with.

---

[2] Beer belly.

"What's your name?" "How long have you been traveling?" etc. etc. etc.

I got so wrapped up in attempting to make new best friends that I lost track of my counting and got so pissed at myself that I let out an audible sigh of frustration.

These people clearly thought I must be nuts.

I aborted my plan to count how many steps it took to be over my head, and decided that was a task for tomorrow. For now, I would frolic in the kiddie-pool sea and work on getting a nice bronzed tan while standing in the middle of the Adriatic Sea.

That evening we were like royalty, making friends with the dining staff, the bartenders, the lifeguards, the live-entertainment which consisted of a local guy named Eni and his cousin, Irisa, who would not only perform, but would go on to teach all the guests the art of traditional Albanian dancing.

Throughout our stay we became friends with the bellhop boys, and the guy that sold you hookah and even the masseuse that gave us our massages, facials, and pedicures.

We were, without a doubt, the king and queen of the Adriatik Hotel.

By the end of our final day there, I even befriended a 12-year old boy that would illegally walk up and down the beach with his coolers selling ice cold beers. Each day, he would walk up to our cabana, ask if we wanted to buy his beers, and he would say to us "Buy from nobody else, only me."

And each day I would say the same thing to him, "We will buy two now. Come back in a half hour and we will buy two more. Then, if you still have any left a half-hour after that, we will take whatever else is left in your cooler so you can go home."

That boy and I took about a million and a half pictures together on our last day there, and even to this day, I often think of him and wonder if he has ever found a better customer.

The Adriatik Hotel was perfect. They had everything one would need to spend four complete days in luxury without ever leaving its confines.

But perhaps the best part about the hotel was its location. I am not referring to the fact that it was sitting on the beach, but the fact that it was directly next door to a casino.

And if there is one thing Erin and I like more than drinking beers and daiquiris on the beach while smoking strawberry and peach flavored hookah in our private cabana, it's gambling.

So on our final night at the Adriatik Hotel, Erin and I decided to do some gambling. It was a "casino" by Albanian standards, meaning it had nothing but slot machines, and was the size of an elementary school classroom, but it got us our fix.

I started playing video poker and was holding my own, which is way more than Erin could say. I am pretty sure she didn't win a single hand. But after about twenty minutes I was up the equivalent of about $5 USD while Erin was feeding the machine more colorful Albanian money.

Then, all of a sudden, the room went black. Sirens started blaring and disco balls fell from the ceiling. The roar of trumpets blared through the tiny casino room. We looked all around to see what the hell was happening. I can only compare it to when the "thunderstorm" strikes when you are dining at a Rainforest Cafe and everyone stops eating their meals to take in all the action.

I saw a man in a suit walking towards me carrying a brown paper bag. Then I looked back at my screen and saw the words "JACKPOT - ALBANIA."

Apparently the country of Albania was running some sort of special promotion all month as an incentive to get people to come into their casinos and gamble away their hard-earned money.

There were "Canino Jackpots," "Local Town/City Jackpots," and the illusive "Albania Jackpot," that were randomly given out to slot machine guests.

I had just won the country of Albania's jackpot.

Cheers ran through the crowd (Erin) as the man came over and handed me the bag full of Albania money and walked away, without so much as a "Congratulations."

I didn't even look inside the bag before I said to Erin, "Let's get the hell out of here."

"Yup," she immediately replied.

We took the bag back to the privacy of our suite and started counting the money, which also contained my other winnings from the slot machine. We counted 90,000 Albanian Lek, which equaled about $800 USD.

I am not proud of the fact that I said something along the lines of "That's it? That is their entire country's JACKPOT?"

It is awesome, and a good chunk of change, but maybe the term "Albania's Jackpot" isn't quite the term they should be using. Maybe "Albania's Big Win," or something, I don't know.

Nevertheless, we celebrated. But the problem was that we were leaving Albania the next day, and converting the money back to USD or the currency of the next country we were visiting seemed like a waste, seeing as the conversion rate would take away much of it.

So, at dinner we got the most expensive meals on the menu. We ordered entrees as appetizers, the finest bottle(s) of wine and multiple delicacies for dessert.

After dinner, I even asked the front desk for our bill from the past three days and paid for it in cash. We even purchased bus tickets to take us to our next destination, Macedonia.

Then we went to the beach bar to spend the rest as we partied the night away.

When we woke up (late) the next morning, we counted the money and realized that we still had a couple hundred dollars worth of Albanian lek left, but we needed to catch our bus down the road, and determined we would have to suck it up and exchange it for Macedonian money when we arrived.

We rushed to the bus stop, yelling our goodbyes to the staff as we ran through the hotel and down the street, hoping our bus didn't leave without us.

Luckily the bus was running late, or so we were told by the 50 or so people that had already gathered for the same journey.

We waited ten minutes. Still no bus.

"I really wish I had just left the rest of this money for tips for all the workers that took such good care of us the past few days," I said to Erin.

"Yeah, that would have been nice, but we ran out of time," she sorrowfully replied.

"Maybe I should run back and give it to all of them," I said.

"NO WAY," she said. "The bus could be here any second," she screamed at me.

So we waited another twenty minutes. Still no bus.

"This is ridiculous," I said, "I feel awful. They were so good to us," I pleaded, begging her to give me the OK to make the run back to the hotel.

"If it is not here in 15 minutes, then run back," she finally agreed.

So I waited. And when there was no sign of the bus after 15 minutes, I threw down my bags, demanded for her to watch them, and said "I will be right back."

"HURRY. THE. HELL. UP," she warned me, "We CAN NOT miss this bus."

"I'LL BE RIGHT BACK," I yelled, already halfway down the road.

I stormed into the Adriatik Hotel like a lightning bolt, first giving money to the bellhop that carried our bags when we arrived. Then hugged him and told him I loved him.

Then I ran to the front desk workers that had made me about 28 new keys during my stay because I kept losing them. I gave them money and told them I loved them.

Then on to the kitchen to find the servers that were preparing for their day. I gave each of them money and told them I loved them.

One last stop… the bartender…

I found him opening up shop for the day, gave him all the rest of the money and said to him "I love you most of all."

We hugged as he said "You must have one final drink. I will make it quick."

"No. I can't," I said. "Erin will murder me if we miss the bus."

"Insistoj," he said to me.

Or in English…

"I insist."

Due to the fact that I have the self control of a chimpanzee, I accepted his offer.

"I will have to drink it real fast," I said, "Then I must go."

"Very fast I will make it," he promised.

Now the term "very fast" is very different throughout the world. In New York City, for example, "very fast," is... well... very fast.

But in Durres, Albania, and much of Europe, and Africa, and Asia, "very fast," does not necessarily mean "I will do it as quickly as I humanly can."

I watched as he sliced a coconut to blend in my Pina Colada. I watched as he searched the entire bar for the pineapple juice he would use for my concoction. And I watched as he meticulously blended my drink, without haste or urgency, as if he was trying to perfect the world's greatest Pina Colada of all time.

Eventually, he handed me my drink, telling me that he, too, loved me and he would miss Mr. Ryan and Ms. Erin so very much.

I promised him we would return some day as I drank my Pina Colada faster than any human has, or should, ever drink a Pina Colada.

I hugged him and thanked him for a perfect four days as I ran away screaming "Love you, love you, love you," to an Albanian bartender I met less than 96 hours earlier.

You don't have to be Sherlock Holmes to come to the conclusion that by the time I got back to Erin she was sitting on her suitcases, all alone at the bus stop. The bus had come and gone.

"You had a drink with Elger, didn't you?" were the first words out of her mouth.

"Yes," I solemnly said.

The next bus didn't leave for Macedonia for another nine hours.

"What the hell are we going to do now?" Erin asked, as we picked up our bags and started aimlessly walking around.

"Well, we could go see our friends at Hotel Adriatik," I said, almost giddy with the fact that I would get some more time with the staff.

Erin agreed that was our best bet, adding "and maybe the casino?"

We walked back into the hotel and were treated as if we were hometown heroes returning from a war in which we received medals of honor.

"Please tell me you have cash left and you didn't give it all away so we can get lunch, a few drinks and play some more slots," Erin said.

I ignored her, walked right to the front desk workers that I had showered with Albanian leks just a few minutes prior, and said "Can you please point me to the closest ATM?"

10. India – Low Budget
भारत में आपका स्वागत है

India. The ultimate travel challenge. Clearly Frank Sinatra never visited the country, because if he did, his iconic song "New York, New York" would have been named "New Delhi, New Delhi." After surviving the complete and utter chaos that is India, one can truly say *if I can make it there, I'll make it anywhere.*

I had done my research on India, and was aware of the challenges that I was going to be facing for my month-long trek across the massive country. I was mentally prepared for the sanitary precautions, I was ready for the long bus journeys and the life threatening tuk tuk rides. And after a weekend drinking and eating as many steins of beer and bratwurst sausages that I could get my hands on in Munich during Oktoberfest with my cousin Paul, I was more than primed to lose a few pounds.

When I landed from Germany and de-boarded the airplane to arrive at the baggage claim, I was bracing for the worst. I was pleasantly surprised when the New Delhi airport was clean, quiet, and shockingly well-organized.

I effortlessly gathered my luggage from the baggage claim and proceeded to the waiting area to kill some time while my friend Jens, a young, ambitious, solo traveler from Switzerland arrived to join me on my Indian adventure.

I met Jens at a hostel in Croatia where he was working for a few months to supplement the costs of traveling. He did not have much in the way of a travel itinerary, but knew he wanted to see as much of the world as possible before returning to the neutral zone that he calls home.

I told him I was heading to India, he mentioned how he has always wanted to visit India, and within minutes of meeting we were both on our computers purchasing our visas. When solo traveling around the world, strangers very quickly become your new best friends and travel companions.

Less than thirty minutes after I was settled in the waiting area, Jens arrived, and in doing so stripped me of my title of "Whitest Person in New Delhi." One thing I learned very quickly during my short wait in the New Delhi airport is that no matter how hard you try to not stick out like a sore thumb in India, you are, inevitably, going to stick out like a sore thumb. I might as well have flown to India wearing my German lederhosen that I wore at Oktoberfest. I swear I would not have stuck out any more than I already was.

Our first task of finding the train to take us to our hostel in central New Delhi proved to be mindless, as conveniently all of the signs that said "train" in Hindi had a picture of a train on them. Regardless, I felt a bit of pride when reaching the train platform, my first task in India was a success.

But the stupid smile slowly faded from my face when I realized that a five-year old could have done what I just did by following the pictures of the "choo choo trains;" quite the humbling thought. I am pretty sure I would still be standing in the New Delhi airport if I had to rely on actually reading anything in Hindi.

I will admit to being more than a little skeptical about taking a train in India. And by "skeptical" I mean, I was shitting my pants. Everything I have ever seen about trains in India was terrifying. Hundreds of people in each section crowded together so tight that there isn't room for an apple to fall. People dangling outside of the train, barely hanging on to the handles as the train carries them along.

I envisioned us trying to get onto the crowded train and not being able to shove ourselves in because of all our luggage. Then I pictured the doors slamming shut on us, and being trampled once the doors finally opened at the next stop as hundreds of Indians were both getting into and off the train at the exact same time. And don't even get me started as to what I imagined this entire experience would smell like.

So you can imagine my relief when the train came down the tracks and I saw exactly zero limbs dangling out of the windows and doors. Then even more relief when the doors opened, and not only was plenty of seating available, but the train was pristine. Compared to a NYC subway, the train from New Delhi airport to central New Delhi was like riding on the Orient Express.

With the stress of dying in an Indian train stampede behind me, my brain now had time to focus on the next possible scenario in which I could endure a horrific death in India; malaria.

When you have a mother like mine, it is difficult to not get a tad bit brainwashed into believing all of her horror stories about traveling. Based on the way my mother was convinced I was going to get malaria the second I stepped off the plane in India you would think that she got her PhD in Malaria Studies from Harvard University and did her thesis on Preventative Actions Against Malaria.

So naturally, I had about three months worth of anti-malarial tablets shoved into all corners of my backpack, along with a dozen or so holy scapulas and palms that are blessed at Palm Sunday mass, which keep multiplying in all of my pieces of luggage every time I travel anywhere. Apparently my mother is convinced these blessed items will prevent my plane from falling out of the sky.

I have had to take anti-malarial pills before and was aware of the potential side-effects, specifically the vivid night terrors that many people experience when taking the medicine. In 2009 when I was in Uganda for the summer, I took a weekly malaria pill which, accordingly to my roommate, prompted me to have full-blown conversations with myself which included both fits of hysteria, as well as literal sobbing. I swear I have a better chance of having a heart attack from the dreams I have when taking anti-malarial pills than I do dying of the mosquito borne illness itself. So I decided to hold off on the malaria pills until I felt like I was in actual danger of getting malaria.

After a twenty minute train ride Jens and I arrived at our stop. I had been very impressed with my first few hours in India, and began to think that all that nervous build up was all for nothing. What is the big deal about traveling in India? This place is a piece of cake. Or dare I say, a piece of gulab jamun (a milk-based Indian dessert.)

Then the train arrived at our destination and we deboarded.

It took one glance at my surroundings to realize what all that "India is complete and utter pandemonium," talk was about. We tried our hardest to look like we knew what the hell we were doing, but very quickly realized we were not fooling anyone. It was madness. No less than fifteen tuk tuk drivers were surrounding us and insisting they take us to our accommodation.

A tuk tuk is India's version of a taxi. It is a motorized rickshaw with three wheels and open to the stale Indian air. A typical tuk tuk can fit about three passengers, or two travelers that are traveling around the world and their massive backpacks they are taking along for the adventure.

We shook them all off and made our way back to the main station to get our bearings and figure out what the hell we were going to do. We asked each and every employee we stumbled upon to point us in the direction of our hostel, which we knew was only a short walk away. The problem, however, was that none of them spoke a lick of English. The only people that seemed to speak English were the pesky tuk tuk drivers. Convenient for them, quite unfortunate for us.

Much like Morocco, one of the things everyone will warn you about before going to India is to watch out for scams. While it is not a dangerous place in terms of being physically attacked or held at gunpoint, it seems as though everyone is out to scam you, or get you to give them money under the umbrella of them "helping you."

From doing my thorough research on India, I was very much aware of this, and vowed to myself that I would not fall victim to the Indian tourist scamming the way I did multiple times in Morocco. After reminding myself and Jens of this, we decided to look for the friendliest looking tuk tuk driver that we could find, and politely ask him how to get to our hostel.

One tuk tuk driver in particular was grinning from ear to ear and seemed to be the life of the tuk tuk driver party, so we approached him and asked if he could tell us how to get to our hostel.

"Of course. Sure. Where are you from?" asked the driver.

"America and Switzerland," we responded, both naming our own country first, which seemed to confuse the young man.

"Can you just show us how to get to our hostel?" we said, showing him screenshots on our phones which had the name of our place.

"Of course. That is only right down that road," he said, pointing in the direction we needed to walk.

"That is great. We will come find you after we get settled in and we will take all our tuk tuk rides with you. Thank you so much," I said, relieved that he was not insisting that we get in his tuk tuk.

We started to walk in the direction he pointed and were only a few steps away when he added, "But you can not get there because it is closed off."

"What do you mean we can not get there? Why is it closed?" I asked.

He responded with one simple word, which nearly dropped me to my knees.

"Malaria."

WHAT? So there is malaria at our hostel right down the road, but there is not malaria right here? What, and how, the actual fuck is that possible? I thought to myself.

"Soooo, ummmmmm," is what I actually said out loud.

"I will take you to a new hotel with no malaria," said the man that all of a sudden didn't seem like the friendliest tuk tuk driver in the world anymore.

"No. We do not need another hotel. We will just get to ours and confirm that they have malaria there, and then figure out if we are going to risk our lives and stay there, or find somewhere in the neighborhood with no malaria," I explained.

Now I know how stupid those words sound, but the Indian people have a hell of a way of making things that are so far fetched sound so reasonable. I can't be sure what actually led me to believe that there was no malaria where I was standing, but if I walked three minutes down the road, my hostel was going to be surrounded with mosquitos that would kill me.

Out of an abundance of caution, I made the hasty, and abominable decision of opening my bag, going into my medical kit, and swallowing not one, but TWO anti-malaria pills. *Not today, killer mosquitos,* I said to myself as I nearly choked to death on the horse tranquilizer-sized pills.

If I am going to give my mother the satisfaction of saying "I told you so," it certainly is not going to be because I contracted malaria my first hour in India.

"But I can bring you to the agency to get clearance to go into the malaria area," our driver then said, which really confused the hell out of us.

"So, there is an agency that will give us a piece of paper that says we can go into our malaria-ridden hostel? Is that what you are saying?" I asked the tuk tuk driver that I was beginning to dislike.

"Yes. Right down the road. I will bring you for free."

There is no bigger red flag in the world than when an Indian tuk tuk driver tells you that he will bring you somewhere for free. I know this now.

Even though it was asinine to believe any of the things he was telling us, we reluctantly did, and allowed him to take us in his tuk tuk to "the agency." As he was driving us, that big smile that drew us to him in the first place, returned, and I remembered why we originally chose him from the sea of drivers begging for our business. He was genuinely friendly, outgoing, and all in all, seemed to be a good guy.

After a harrowing ride zipping through New Delhi on our tuk tuk we arrived at "the agency," which was basically just a travel agency. Not basically, it *was* a travel agency.

The owner of the agency would no doubt be a slimey, weasely, used car salesman if he lived in the United States, and after taking one look at him, I knew that I was not going to fall for anything he was telling us.

He sat us down, took out his notepad and asked us about our travel itinerary.

How long would we be in India? What other cities are we planning on visiting? What excursions are we looking to experience? What attractions do we want to visit? Where are we staying in each destination?

I started to briefly answer the questions, then stopped, and said "Can we just get that pass that allows us to go to our hostel with malaria, please?"

He looked at me the way you would look at anyone that said that to *you*; confused.

"Excuse me? What pass?" said the creepy travel agent.

"Our tuk tuk driver said we needed a pass to get to our hostel because it is in a malaria zone. We do not need any help planning our trip, it is all planned out," I lied.

He kept trying to offer us deals on hotels without malaria, and trains that were "way more comfortable" than the ones we told him we would be taking.

But at each offer, I said "No thank you. We are definitely not buying anything."

He was clearly pissed that he wasn't going to make any money off of us, and said "You can go, you do not need a pass to get into the malaria hostel. It will be fine. I will make a call."

After wasting a solid hour in the agency that we didn't even need to go to, we got back in the tuk tuk and our driver said "Did you buy anything?" hoping that he would soon be receiving a nice commission sum from the agency.

"No. And we didn't even need the malaria pass, imagine that," I said, as sarcastically as my voice would allow.

"Bring us to our malaria hostel please," I asked.

"OK, but it is 1200 rupees," the driver said.

"WHAT, that is outrageous! You are the one that said we needed to come here when we didn't even have to," Jens screamed in his Swiss-English, or as I like to call it, Swinglish.

"It's fine. I'll pay it. Let's just get to this hostel so I can either take a shower and relax, or just die of malaria and not have to deal with tuk tuk drivers and travel agents anymore," I moaned.

When we arrived at the hostel there was not a mosquito in sight and there was no sign of a road blockade at all. And shockingly enough, there was not even a sign that said "Malaria zone begins here."

We explained the incident to our hostel staff and they laughed and said "No malaria here. That is silly."

Good enough for me. *Crisis averted,* I thought to myself.

After showering and changing into the most Indian wardrobe I could find (my Moroccan shirt that I got swindled into buying in Morocco) we were off to the city center, which was either a 20 minute walk, or a two minute tuk tuk ride. Seeing as we both hadn't eaten anything, and were famished, we opted for the time saving tuk tuk ride.

We asked our driver to bring us to the city center to the restaurant our hostel worker recommended for us.

"Ok, I will bring you for free," said our new tuk tuk driver, "We will just make one quick stop first."

"Oh hell no, we have already been to the travel agency. Just bring us to the restaurant. We will pay. DO NOT BRING US TO THE AGENCY," I demanded.

He reluctantly agreed to bring us directly to our restaurant and we handed him more than enough rupees for the short ride. He was happy with the generous tip, and we were happy to avoid the agency.

We indulged in our first Indian dinner. Actually Jens indulged in his first TWO Indian dinners. My fried vegetable noodle dish was way too spicy for my delicate taste buds, so I had about three bits, slid the plate over to him, and flagged the server down to order a beer (I originally ordered bottled water with my meal, not a beer. It was too hot for beer. That is the only way to describe how oppressively steaming it was.)

The waiter came over and apologetically said that they were not serving beer because today is a "dry day."

"A dry day?" I managed to utter. "What does this mean? Like EVERYWHERE is dry today?" I said, unable to hide the panic in my voice.

"Yes. It is Gandhi's birthday. Everyone is dry today. No alcohol sales at all," the waiter explained.

I sat there like a bratty child that could not get their way and waited for Jens to finish our meals.

When we left dinner I popped my head into every store and restaurant I passed and said "No beer today, right?" Each and every person confirmed the horror; today was a bone dry day in India.

As we began the walk home, defeated, we passed a polite, older Indian gentleman in a business suit. He smiled at us, and said "Welcome to India, where are you from? How long will you be here?"

We each told him our stories, and he seemed genuinely interested. He began to walk with us and asked us where we were walking. We told him we were heading back to our hostel because today is a dry day and nobody was selling beer.

"Oh, I know a place where you can get beer, follow me," the man excitedly announced.

At that point he could have been leading me into a lion's den and I still would have followed him. It was over 100 degrees, I had been traveling for about 20 straight hours from Germany, and I really wanted a damn cold beer. So we followed him through the streets that were for some reason becoming more and more familiar.

Finally, he opens the door to the place that would give us beers. Sitting there, with his same slimey, up-to-no-good look on his face, was the "travel agent" we encountered hours earlier.

"You would like to buy my train tickets now?" he said excitedly.

"No, we are here because this man said we could get a beer here," I said.

"Oh yes. Sit down. We can do that," he said casually, pulling out the same pamphlets and maps he used as props the first time we were in his office.

And just like that, he begins going through new transportation options, accommodations, and activities for us to do while in India. We couldn't get a word in edgewise.

After about twenty minutes of listening to him ramble on, while sitting in the dark, musty cubicle in the dirty office, we interrupted him and said, "Can we just get that beer? We still do not need any travel help from you. Will pay for the beer and leave."

"Today is dry day in India. We no have beer," said my least favorite human being in the world.

We looked at each other, stunned that we somehow ended up in the same travel agency two times within hours, stood up and walked out the door. As we began the trek back to our malaria-free hostel, I was excited to finally get into bed and get a good night of sleep after such a long day.

… until I remembered that I took not one, but two anti-malarial pills that will surely be producing some doubly horrific night terrors, more than likely including that God awful travel agency and cringeworthy salesman.

11. India - Moderate Budget
The Holiest High

Varanasi, India is widely considered to be one of the holiest places on Earth. Located directly on the Ganges River, devout Hindus from all over the world will come to Varanasi to die.

Yes, you read that correctly.

It is believed that if you die and are cremated in the holy city, and your ashes scattered in the Ganges River, you will achieve moksha, a blissful state of existence and the liberation from being reincarnated. Basically if you die in Varanasi, you will not pass go, you will not collect $200, but you will instead go directly to nirvana.

There are even hotels in Varanasi that will only accept you if you are planning to die within the next 14 days. If the guests do not pass away within those two weeks, they must check out and their bed will be given to someone else; it is basically their way of telling their dying customers to shit or get off the pot.

This may sound morbid to many Westerners, but it is actually quite reasonable when you understand that these Indian people are trying to obtain moksha and believe they will become liberated from the trials and tribulations of life, on their deathbeds. This ensures their souls will be free, they will stop being reincarnated, and finally achieve guru status. A guru is someone that has achieved nirvana, meaning they fully understand the relationship between god and man and instead of reincarnation, they will be able to enjoy the afterlife.

Whether or not you choose to die in one of these "death hotels," (which is eerily similar to what I call every hotel on the strip in Las Vegas when I am violently hungover and attempting to check out) when someone dies in Varanasi their bodies are burned next to the Ganges and their ashes are dispersed into the holy river in a beautiful, religious ritual.

In addition to being considered one of the holiest cities in the world, Varanasi is also known to be one of the best places to experience the religious festival of Holi. Holi is the popular ancient Hindu festival that many refer to as the Festival of Colors. While it is considered a religious celebration, it also signifies the beginning of spring, the end of winter, and the blossoming of love. It is used by locals as a time to "forgive and forget" and to repair broken relationships.

During the festival, buckets and water guns filled with colored water and colored powder are tossed carelessly around the city and over its patrons until everybody becomes one like nature; filled with spring color. When the celebration is over and the people wash the colors off their bodies, they are symbolically washing away their sins.

Joy and laughter ring through the streets as old grudges are settled, and new relationships bloom. Many traditions are revisited during each yearly festival, the most interesting being the distribution of the cannabis-infused Indian drink, bhang lassi. The drink is known to be very potent. Just ask any hippy you know and they will tell you all about the bhang lassi milkshake, as many hippies travel from all over the world to get their hands on them.

The use of cannabis in Indian culture dates back to around 2000 BC. If you're keeping track at home, that is about 2000 years before Jesus. Speaking of Jesus, many scholars even believe that cannabis was a main ingredient in the sacred anointing oil that God directed Moses to whip up in Exodus 30: 23 - 25. Go research it and decide for yourself. Just Google something like "Did Jesus use pot," and you should have all the information you need to make an informative decision.

The cannabis drink is consumed by Hindus during the Holi festival in order to pay their respects to Shiva, widely considered to be their supreme god. Legend has it that once Shiva discovered the plant, it became his favorite food, and he would consume it quite often to help meditate and relax. They believe that the drink will help them better understand and worship their Hindu god.

At other times throughout the year there are government authorized Bhang shops, which serve the delicious bhang lassi milkshake. Many times it will simply be referred to as a "special lassi." The drink is made with yogurt, nuts, spices, rose water, and of course, cannabis. The amount of cannabis the milkshake contains is entirely up to you, as they offer weak, moderate, strong, and very strong options. Basically the rule of thumb is if you want to relax, order a weak one, if you want to slip into a weeklong coma order a very strong one.

The locals in Varanasi are some of the friendliest people I have met around the world. They will spend hours sitting on the steps overlooking the Ganges River just talking to you and learning about your life, and what path led you to their holy city.

Each night we would step out of our hotel and take a stroll along the Ganges, chatting with locals about their culture and traditions. On our last night in Varanasi a local man, Muhammed, began talking to us about the Holi festival, which led to the discussion about the distribution of the bhang lassi milkshake.

We were intrigued by this "religious" cannabis drink and expressed our disappointment that we were not in Varanasi during the time the Holi festival takes place. He then shared with us the fact that bhang lassi milkshakes are available at select government authorized restaurants and cafes throughout the year and he would be happy to walk us there.

What kind of travel writer would I be if I didn't partake in consuming the holiest drink in one of the holiest places on Earth, right?

We agreed to meet at noon the next day. One would imagine that should give us plenty of time for the drink to wear off before our 6:00 p.m., 13-hour bus ride to Udaipur. Spoiler alert: it wasn't.

So the next day, after packing up our bags and leaving them at the front desk, we headed out to meet Muhammad so he can lead us to our bhang lassi milkshakes. The cafe was just a few buildings down from our hotel, which was in a prime area of Varanasi. Luckily I was traveling in Varanasi on a moderate budget, so I didn't need to skimp out on accommodations, as many of the accommodation options we passed looked to be downright daunting.

Back in 1897 legendary author Mark Twain wrote about his experiences in Varanasi, which is also sometimes referred to as Benares…

"Benares (Varanasi) is older than history, older than tradition, older even than legend and looks twice as old as all of them put together."

What a hoot, that Mark Twain. But he is right, I would not be surprised if Varanasi was literally older than dirt. It makes Rome look like it was just the subject of an episode of Extreme Makeover: City Edition.

So with that being said, I was thankful to be staying in a hotel that was relatively new. And by "new," I mean it was built in 1870 and converted into the hotel it is today in 1990.

Anyway, when we arrived at the bhang lassi shop my anxiety was through the roof. I have survived Indian transportation, Indian food and successfully avoided malaria for nearly two weeks, the last thing I wanted to do was die from a cannabis milkshake in Varanasi, India. They are so cremation happy there that my body would be turned into little pieces of floating ash before the sun was even down. Hell, I would even wake up extra early when I was in Varanasi because I was fearful that if the maid service came in at noon and saw me still in bed, she would assume I was dead and bring in the firestarters.

So when the man at the bhang lassi stand asked me the strength of the milkshake I said "Weak. Very weak."

My travel companion Jens, however, opted for the strong bhang lassi, much to my disapproval.

So the man made us one weak bhang lassi and one strong bhang lassi and I didn't take my eyes off of the two milkshakes from the second he started making them. I have heard nightmares about the strong bhang lassi milkshakes and am confident that if our drinks somehow ended up switched around I would literally start floating away if I took even one sip.

"These milkshakes *better* not get switched around," I warned Jens. "I would like to stay right here, with two feet solidly planted on the 76 billion year old Varanasi dirt."

After questioning the man harder than the FBI questions suspected murderers and making him confirm a dozen times that the milkshake I was holding in my hand was the very weak lassi, I paid him for my bhang lassi (about $2 USD) and took my first sip.

It was delicious. If I didn't know there was cannabis in the drink, I would have gulped it down faster than an Irish-American college student gulps down shots of Jameson on St. Patrick's Day and ordered another one.

But because I am a responsible adult that always puts safety first, I had about two thirds of my "weak," bhang lassi and was about to leave the rest on the counter when Jens yelled at me and told me he would finish mine. Swiss kids don't mess around.

So we headed home and waited for the bhang lassi to kick in. According to the research I did, it should take about an hour to start feeling any effects from the drink, and the effects would last a few hours. If I planned accordingly, I would be just fine by the time we needed to leave for the bus station.

When we arrived back at our hotel, we went to the rooftop and let the waiting game begin. Jens and I agreed we didn't feel anything and we were convinced we had been duped, yet again, in India. No sooner had we said this when Jens pointed to the Ganges River, directly across the street from us, and said "Whoa, look at those kites. They are flying and they don't have any strings attached!"

"Oh my God," I shrieked. "Who is controlling them and how are they making them dip down into the water and then go back up into the sky?" I asked, wildly impressed.

"I have no idea. They must be battery operated and have some sort of remote control," Jens replied.

"That is so amazing. String-less kites. What will they think of next?" I said, lounging back and taking in the beautiful view of the Ganges and the fascinating magical kites that appeared just in time to wish us farewell to the holy city.

"Let's walk down and see who is controlling them," Jens begged.

"Maybe we should stay here in case the bhang lassi starts to kick in," I said. "I don't want to be down on the river after a bhang lassi. Too many people we would have to talk to."

"You're right," Jens agreed, and we proceeded to sit in silence, staring at the kites for what seemed to be an eternity, reflecting on an unforgettable time in Varanasi, and taking mental notes of how special of a place it is.

An hour later it was time to head to the bus station. When we collected our bags from the front desk we expressed our fascination with the string-less kites to the worker.

"I do not know what you are talking about," said the teenage clerk. "Nobody has battery operated kites here. We are very poor."

We assured him we knew what we were seeing and told him to follow us outside to see for himself. Once outside we pointed to the kites and said "See? We told you."

"Those are not battery operated, string-less kites", he said, "That is just garbage floating around."

We instantly realized that we were not duped by the bhang lassi man, and learned just how well these milkshakes work.

We gathered our bags from the front desk worker and asked a tuk tuk driver to deposit us at the bus station so we could catch our ride to Udaipur, laughing quite literally the entire way. That tuk tuk driver probably still tells stories about the happiest people he has ever met in his life.

Then we arrived at the bus station just in time for full-fledged bhang lassi "holiness."

Many "bus stations" in Varanasi, and much of India are just stops along the side of the road. And when our tuk tuk driver stopped at a window and told us this is where we buy our tickets, we were uncertain and questioned silently to each other if he brought us to the right place. But because of our bhang lassis, we decided we didn't really care and got out anyway.

We went to the window and paid the nice lady behind the counter our $6 USD each for the 13-hour bus ride to Udaipur, and she told us we could wait on the steps outside. The bus would be here soon.

So when the bus didn't arrive after 20 minutes, Jens started to panic. He did, after all, have a strong bhang lassi as well as a third of a weak bhang lassi.

I was too busy floating through the galaxy to notice how much time had passed. But seeing how nervous he was that we were in the wrong place I went up to the lady and asked her to confirm that we were where we needed to be. I made sure that the bus was indeed coming, and that we would be able to see the bus when it arrived. All questions, which she answered clearly just 20 minutes prior.

So I sat back down and waited. To check and see how much the bhang lassi had worn off I started to play a little game with myself. I was staring at the spot in between two parked buses across the street and going through the alphabet trying to name my favorite band that began with every letter of the alphabet… Aerosmith. Blink 182. Counting Crows, etc... If I could get to ZZ Top (which I hate but it is the only band I can think of that starts with a "Z"), without getting distracted, that means I am no longer crippled by the effects of the special milkshake.

Not long after I said "Foo Fighters" I noticed a woman walking through the spot I was staring at. She was walking backwards, with a broom, sweeping the road. Immediately after I saw another woman, also walking backwards, in the opposite direction, doing the same thing.

What is this the fucking opening scene of "Stomp: The Musical? I said out loud. I was clearly still "on the bhang" because I then proceeded to laugh so hard at my own joke that I ended up in a coughing fit, unable to catch my breath.

The only thing that calmed me down was the sobering fact that if I don't catch my breath soon, I am going to faint right on these Varanasi steps, and the only person I know in this entire country, sitting right next to me, is currently completely and utterly useless. I swear I could have dropped dead, they could lit a bonfire and thrown my body in it, and tossed my remains in the Ganges, and Jens still would have been unaware anything was happening.

I finally regained my composure from my own hysterical joke just in time for Jens to snap out of his coma, glance over at me and whisper "Is the bus coming?" in the exact same tone the little boy in the movie *The Sixth Sense* whispers "I See Dead People."

Paranoia breeds paranoia, so I mustered up the coordination to stand up, walk to the window and ask the same lady the same questions, this time adding, "But will the bus see us?"

"Yes," she insisted. "You are in the right place. The bus is coming. You will see the bus. And the bus will see you."

"Ok. Great. Sorry to bother you again," I said. I started to walk away before stopping and adding, "But just to be safe, do you think you can let me know when the bus is here?"

God, I was feeling "holy."

I returned to my seat, trying not to think about the ladies walking backwards towards each other, sweeping in unison. But then I saw them down the road, still sweeping, and imagined them breaking out with their rendition of Annie's "It's a Hard Knock Life" and started laughing again. All by myself.

Then I was distracted by something else. This being India and all I was not surprised to see a donkey walk right past my feet.

Huh, that's a cute donkey, I remember thinking, as if it looked any different from any other donkey in the world.

Then another donkey walked by.

Whoa, another cute donkey! I said, out loud this time.

Then, out of nowhere, a herd of donkeys came walking by. I would estimate about 50 donkeys, all just going for a Sunday stroll on a busy Indian road. No human herding them along or anything. Totally normal, right?

Just when the procession of donkeys had gone by, I remember thinking that I would have loved to have taken a picture of those donkeys, but unfortunately my brain was still not properly allowing my limbs to receive direct messages, and was therefore physically unable to take my backpack off, unzip my bag, and figure out how to work a camera.

I returned to my "favorite band" game to patiently wait for our bus… Nirvana… Oasis, Pearl Jam, etc., until I looked to my right and saw two final donkeys coming around the corner. They were baby donkeys. Left completely unattended. They slowly walked down the road that their friends had walked down many minutes before. They were in no rush. They were playing with each other, banging their heads into each other and nudging each other along.

I watched as the two cutest donkeys I had ever seen playfully walked past me. I remember hoping that they would always be happy, playful donkeys, even when they got to be older. This bhang lassi stuff is amazing, isn't it?

About five minutes passed and I was still silently obsessing over the two baby donkeys.

Then, out loud, I yelled "Those two should really stop donkey'ing around and catch up with their friends."

I then proceeded to violently scream at the top of my lungs in laughter, even awakening Jens out of whatever universe he was in at the time.

Moments later, after congratulating myself countless times for being the funniest person alive, the bus finally arrived as I was still damn near hyperventilating from my donkey joke. I re-confirmed with the poor worker lady that this was indeed the bus we needed to get on, and she happily waved us goodbye.

When I tucked myself into my bed on the overnight bus to Udaipur I was sad to be leaving Varanasi, but made a mental note to add "Attend the Holi Festival in Varanasi," to my bucket list.

But that would have to wait until tomorrow. I was still feeling way, way too "holy" to be writing anything at the moment.

12. India - Luxury Budget
I Told You This Wasn't a Good Idea

After 39 years of having to deal with my own stupidity, I have become quite good at learning from my mistakes. I know what I am good at and I know my weaknesses.

For example, no matter how famished I may feel, I know that I am incapable of finishing an entire meal that I order at a restaurant. I take after my beloved grandfather in the fact that I can "eat like a bird, and drink like a fish." So I have learned to either split a meal, or order a smaller portioned meal, such as an appetizer. I am pretty sure if I was ever unfortunate enough to be on death row my final meal would be two beers, one slice of cheese pizza, and a bag of gourmet jelly beans for dessert. With a bottle of fine wine as a nightcap / lifecap.

I also know how abysmal I am with my sense of direction. I swear I could go on a jog around my childhood neighborhood which I have lived in since 1980 and if I get distracted for a few seconds I basically need to fire a distress signal because I am so lost.

I know that I tend to buy an incredible amount of shit that I don't need on Amazon, so now, after making a purchase, I no longer allow myself to look at the "You might also want to buy" or the "Other users that bought this item also bought these items" sections of the site. I now force myself to close out of the site the second I see the confirmation that my purchase was successful.

And finally, I know how God-awful I am at motorized vehicles. To be fair, I am even awful at non-motorized vehicles, such as bikes and skateboards. The popular cliche, "It's like riding a bike" does not apply to me. I am erratic, can't ride in a straight line to save my life, and despite being in what I consider to be decent shape, have to get off and walk the bike up even the slightest incline. Basically anything with wheels I should avoid at all costs.

Even in my car, I would estimate that about 60% of the time that I am getting gas or at a drive thru window I am either way too far away from the gas filling station or the drive thru window employee that I can't reach, or right on top of the gas pumping machine and can't open the door. I basically have to do a six point turn every time I order a Whopper Jr. (which, as we all now know, I am not going to be able to finish anyway.)

Don't even get me started on parallel parking.

So while traveling on a luxury budget in Udaipur, India my travel companion Jens and I were staying at a more upscale hotel. While the comfort level and service were beyond traditional India standards, the problem was that the hotel was a bit outside of the city center. This meant that we had to hire a tuk tuk to take us to any sights or attractions we wanted to visit.

So Jens had the bright idea that maybe we should rent motorbikes for our time in Udaipur. This would allow us to explore more of the city at our own pace, and have a bit more freedom with our allotted time.

"Ohh, I do not know about that," I replied, "I can't ride a motorized vehicle down a desolate Kansas road, which is flatter than a pancake, without crashing. Nevermind driving a motorbike on the roads in India where I am not even sure there are rules about how or where you can drive," I explained.

Not only do I have to watch out for cars, tuk-tuks, and thousands of other motorbikes, but also all the animals that Indians share their road with. When you are at a stoplight in India, you can look to your left and see a cow sitting next to you, and look to your right and see an elephant. I swear I feel like I am smack in the middle of the opening scene of *The Lion King* when King Mufasa is presenting his newborn son, Simba, on Pride Rock, and every animal in the kingdom comes from near and far to meet their new prince, every time I am at a stoplight in India.

"Oh come on, you'll be fine. We will go slow. And aren't you the one that keeps saying how sick you are of tuk tuk drivers trying to swindle us," said my Swiss friend.

And that's really all it took for me to go from "Safety first," to "Safety fifth."

We had our concierge call the motorbike company and order us two of their finest motorbikes for a three day rental. I channeled my inner Harley Davidson and started to mentally prepare for my Indian motorbike debut.

I even got on one of the bicycles that the hotel offered its guests and practiced on it, pretending the handlebars were the actual gas pedal, like on a real motorbike. I received more than a few odd looks as I was making the "Vroom Vroom" sound with my mouth as I sat idle on a bicycle outside the entrance to our hotel.

It wasn't until the motorbikes arrived in our hotel's parking lot that I remembered just how incapable I am at riding them. As the owner of the bikes sat us down to fill out paperwork and take our money, I looked at Jens and said "Maybe I shouldn't do this. I am not sure if I properly managed to express to you just how bad I am at this type of stuff."

"It is too late now. He is here," Jens shot back at me, not even taking his eyes off of his paperwork. His enthusiasm and excitement to ride a motorbike through the streets of India somehow made me think that this might not be the worst idea I have ever agreed to.

I began to fill out my paperwork, all the while thinking that this is definitely not going to end well. I made sure to put my father's name as my emergency contact, because he would probably be able to deal with the initial shock of receiving a call saying that his son died by smashing into the rear end of an elephant while on a motorbike in the streets of India, a little bit better than my mother would be able to handle it.

When I got to question three, "Do you have experience riding a motorbike?" I stopped dead in my tracks.

"Well, technically, yes, I do have experience. Not GOOD experiences, but experiences, nevertheless," I thought to myself.

I told the man that was renting us the motorbikes that I am not too skilled with motorbikes, and quite frankly, have not had the best experiences with motorized vehicles in the past.

You would think, and I was hoping, this would be a red flag for the man, and question whether or not I should be riding the chaotic streets of India on his new, unblemished motorbike.

"It is fine. You will be fine," said the Indian man that was clearly much more concerned about receiving my money than he was about my safety or the safety of his motorbike, "You can practice in the back parking lot before you go onto the streets."

After quite literally signing my life away for the motorbike, I went outside to get some practice. I got on the bike, strapped on my helmet, and gave the bike, what I thought would be just enough gas to get me going slowly on my way. Apparently I have no idea how much gas a motorbike needs to get going, because I shot off faster than a boulder being catapulted at an opposing army in a season finale episode of *Game of Thrones*.

I was going so fast that I swear if I was being filmed, the footage could be used in some sort of Evel Knievel documentary with me playing the starring role of the iconic motorbike-riding daredevil. Except, of course, for the fact that I was screaming "Whoa, whoaaaaa, whoaaaaaaa, whoa, whoaaaaa" as I was frantically trying to gain control of the motorbike.

I eventually found a speed that was adequate for my motorbike riding ability (about 5 mph) and did a few laps around the parking lot, getting in about seven full Hail Mary's along the way.

By the grace of God (and Mary) I made it back to the front lot where Jens, the motorbike renter, and two of his employees were waiting for me. The employees were the ones that actually drove the motorbikes to the hotel, and he would give them a ride back to their shop after we rode off on the death traps.

"Hey, look at you, you made it! How was it?" yelled Jens, beaming with pride that I was still alive.

"I hated it. I hated every single second of it," I said. Looking out into the streets of Udaipur I once again said to my audience, "I am not sure about this. I don't think I should be doing this."

"No way man. Once you get out of this area, and get over that bridge, you will be fine. It is so easy," said the owner of the bikes.

"A BRIDGE! Nobody said anything about a bridge!" I yelled, as I had yet a new image in my head about how I would die in India; plunging to my death off a bridge.

This fell on deaf ears, however, as everyone just ignored my newest excuse to not ride the motorbike.

Jens put on his helmet and began driving onto the road, pulling over to the side to wait for me to build up the courage to leave the hotel parking lot.

"Ok, but I am just telling you, this is not a good idea," I said to the owner, who I can only imagine was daydreaming about how he was going to spend all the money he just squeezed out of the two of us.

"You can do it, my friend!" yelled one of the Indian employees watching on from the sidelines.

Ok, screw it. Here goes nothing…

I again went from 0-60 mph in seconds, but this time, instead of having the time and space to attain a safe speed, I had something stop me… the stomach of the man that rented me the motorbike.

I drove right into his gut at full speed, knocking him to the ground, with me, and the motorbike right on top of him. With my hands still on the handles and the engine still revving, the two employees rushed over to remove the motorbike from on top of us.

While I was still lying there, on top of him, I didn't even apologize for running him over. But I did manage to whisper "I told you this wasn't a good idea."

After we got up and brushed ourselves off, I said "Yeah, I don't think I am going to take the bike. I will just ride on the back of him," pointing to Jens, who was doubled over in a fit of laughter.

"Yes. That is a very good idea," said the man that I just ran over.

After refunding me my money and having one of his employees ride the motorbike back to the shop, the man looked at Jens and said "Good luck with him," before getting into his car and driving away.

We spent the next three days exploring the beautiful city of Udaipur, India nestled together on the back of one motorbike. Just two grown, white men huddled on the back of a motorbike in India.

As if we needed anything else to help us to stick out from the crowd.

13. Sri Lanka - Low Budget Catch of the Day

If India isn't your cup of tea, might I suggest visiting their island neighbor to the south, known for their beautiful beaches, incredible wildlife, and, well… tea.

Not only did I convince Jens to make the journey to Sri Lanka with me, but I also managed to persuade our roommate in a hostel in Mumbai, Joss, to come with us. Picture in your mind, a young, wavy haired, football (soccer) playing lad from the UK. That's Joss. Despite being the quintessential British footy player, Joss is laid back, level headed, and as responsible as someone that decides they are going to travel around India for two months alone with no plans or itinerary could possibly be. A much needed addition to Jens and I.

Although, the only thing that makes two extremely white backpackers traveling around India stick out in the crowd even more, is three extremely white backpackers traveling around Sri Lanka. It really is the beginning of a joke; an American, a Swiss, and a British lad walk into a Sri Lankan bar…

Much like India, travel in Sri Lanka can be incredibly cheap, so instead of paying $5 USD to stay in a crowded hostel, we opted to get a triple room at a hotel right on the beach in Tangalle, Sri Lanka for $$6 USD each. This small hotel was actually purchased by a British couple that stayed there a few years back for their honeymoon. While they were there they fell in love with the place. Towards the end of their trip they noticed a "For sale" sign, joked that they should buy the building, and before they knew it, they actually purchased it and renovated it into the hotel it is today.

When I say "Right on the beach," I mean the waves just about come up to your door. When you step out of your room, you are actually standing on the beautiful white sandy beach staring out into the crystal clear blue water. For just a few dollars a night, you are quite literally staying in paradise.

So when the crashing of waves woke me up around 7:00 a.m. I decided that instead of forcing myself to try and get more sleep, I would start my day by taking a swim in the ocean and get a headstart on lounging in a hammock while sipping three dollar Pina Coladas all day. After a chaotic month in India I was more than primed to get some much needed relaxation.

So without waking the guys, I threw on my swimming trunks, grabbed a towel and *The Catcher in the Rye* (which I basically could recite on my own because I have read it damn near 90 times) and headed out to my backyard; the pristine beaches of Tangalle. My first day in Sri Lanka was going to be epic.

Not even the hotel employees were in sight when I emerged from my room, set up my hammock, and ran full speed into the refreshing ocean. I looked back at the seemingly desolate hotel, and thought to myself, *this place is closer to paradise than anywhere I have ever been. I never want to leave.* I instantly understood why that British couple bought the place on a whim.

I would estimate I was in the water for about 45 seconds before I heard commotion coming from a group of people about 200 yards down the beach. They were all screaming at me, waving their arms above their heads, and yelling "GET OUT!" "HURRY!" "COME HERE!"

Looking down the coast I saw not a single person in the water. Was I about to be eaten by a shark? Was there a deadly man-o-war in the water ready to attack? Hell, I am in Sri Lanka, it could be the friggin loch-ness monster I am frolicking in the water with for all I know.

So I started running out of the water. Let me tell you, there is absolutely no way to look cool running full speed out of the ocean. You can look like a champion running full speed INTO the ocean, but you cannot run full speed OUT of the ocean without looking like a newly inspired, severely out of shape older woman on her first night in a jazzercise class that is way outside of her jazzercise abilities.

Now I am scared for my life, *and* embarrassed that a group of people are watching my pathetic attempt to get out of the water as quick as possible.

Oh my God! I suddenly realized, *it's Sri Lanka, a tsunami is coming*! That is why they are screaming at me to get out.

But after looking back, I was relieved when I saw no signs of a tsunami approaching. No tidal wave on the horizon. Not even a sign of a rip curl. What the hell is going on?

I finally waddled out of the water and started to run to the crowd. As I was running, I was reverted back to my five year career as a surf lifeguard. With every step I was trying to remember all the basics that I may need to save whoever is clearly dying a few yards away.

It wasn't until I got about 20 yards away that I noticed they were all holding onto one of two ropes and pulling it in unison, every person grunting with effort and pain at each pull. I swear I looked in all directions for camera crews because it looked exactly like I just stumbled upon the first immunity challenge on an episode of *Survivor: Sri Lanka.* After seeing no signs of reality TV producers, I asked an English speaking couple what the hell was going on?

"We do not know, but we walked by here as we were on our morning walk and these people made us grab the rope and start pulling. You need to help us," they pleaded.

Once the Sri Lankan men saw me standing there, they all started yelling at me. "Pull. Pull. Pull. Pull."

Not knowing if I was pulling the rope to gain access to a treasure chest, a shark, or a dead body, I began to pull with all my might.

I can honestly say, with every ounce of sincerity, that I never exerted that much energy in my life so early in the morning.

As I began running backwards with the rope in hand, the Australian couple that I first spoke to let go of the rope and both of them collapsed to the ground.

"Thanks so much for coming. This is exhausting," they said.

"What the hell am I pulling this for?" I asked, already feeling like I, too, was going to be collapsing to the ground at any moment.

"We are not too sure, but the man that stopped us said they will give us the best lunch we have ever had with all of the stuff we catch. So we are assuming we are pulling in a load of fish," the Aussies explained to me.

"Ok. Well, I am on a low budget for the next four days. A delicious, fresh, free lunch would be fantastic. This should be over soon, right? I mean, how much farther out can it be?"

What a stupid question if you think about it. We are pulling something that is in the ocean. It could quite literally be hundreds of miles away, I realize in retrospect.

Over the next hour the three of us foreigners took turns helping the men pull this mammoth net into shore. Each of us dripping with sweat, begging for water, and complaining that we could not pull much longer.

After an hour passed, we asked the only local man that spoke any semblance of English how much longer this was going to take. We lied and said we had plans, and had to get going soon.

"Very soon now," the man replied.

He lied.

Another forty-five minutes later we finally saw the first signs of the net. Our reward was in sight. All three of us found the energy to pull with all our might, until finally, the net exploded onto shore, along with thousands of fish.

To be honest, it could have been a net full of gold, with each man allowed to grab as much as he could, and I still would have collapsed to the ground and been unable to grab any gold for myself. I was completely spent.

The three of us hugged, thanked each other for the support, and laid panting in the sun for a solid ten minutes. Only then did I see Joss casually strolling down the beach, completely oblivious to what was happening. He reached us, gave a few tugs on the rope to help the fishermen pull the catch in even further from the waves, and said "What the hell happened to you?"

"You better not get a free lunch for that little tug," was all I was able to say as he helped me to my feet.

The "English speaking" local man came over to us and said they needed to collect, organize and distribute the fish. If we came back at 11:00 a.m. we could have our well deserved reward.

So I stumbled back to my hammock and ordered myself a Pina Colada. Yes, your math is correct, it was like 10:00 a.m.. You try pulling in 20 tons of fish at the first sign of sunlight in Sri Lankan heat, then you can judge me for ordering a Pina Colada for breakfast.

Like Indians, Sri Lankans are on their own time. I could have swam to Thailand by the time my Pina Colada arrived. Apparently, what happened was after I ordered the drink, the workers went to the store to buy the ingredients without telling me.

A half hour passed… no Pina Colada.

An hour passed… no Pina Colada.

I couldn't even focus on reading a paragraph of my book without checking behind me to see if the Pina Colada was coming. Every time I went to ask about it, the workers kept saying "It is coming. It is coming very soon."

The irony that this is the most frustrated that I had been on my trip so far was not lost on me. My frolicking in the ocean was cut short to be forced to be a fisherman for the morning. My hands were blistered and bleeding from pulling the rope. And now I was being denied my much-deserved Pina Colada.

Finally, just as it was time to head to lunch on the beach, my Pina Colada arrived. I drank it in two gulps, spilling ⅓ of it on my chest in all my haste. I jumped in the ocean to wash the frozen concoction off my body and as I did, I heard "Let's go, America! We are all waiting for you!" (Oftentimes when you are traveling internationally, you will simply be referred to as your country when other travelers don't know, or can't remember your name. Which is often.)

I yelled back to Joss and Jens "So long suckers, I am going to my free lunch," and Baywatch'd it again down to the scene of the fish slaughtering. This time instead of thinking I was going to have to perform CPR on someone, I knew what awaited me at the end of my run; a delicious, freshly prepared lunch, made from all our hard work.

"Right down here. Follow me, America," said the English speaking Sri Lankan, as he led us down a dirt road that connected to the main road.

"I thought we were eating on the beach. Should I go put on a shirt? Or shoes? Or get a towel and dry off?" I said, confused about where the man was leading us.

"No. No. What you are wearing (a wet bathing suit) is very fine," the Sri Lankan man said firmly.

So we followed him. The Australian couple had gone to their hotel and changed. I, however, was dripping wet, and wearing only a bathing suit.

The white, sandy beach slowly transformed into a dirt road filled with jagged, pointy rocks, which due to the approaching midday sun, became hotter and hotter with each step on my sensitive bare feet.

Ouch... ouch... ouch... I mumbled each step as my eyes scanned the road ahead of me, searching for what looked like the least painful next step.

The "English speaking" Sri Lankan man then handed us over to a non-English speaking Sri Lankan man. Apparently it was his house that we were going to have our lunch. And without even saying goodbye to us, the "English speaking" man disappeared into an alley and we never saw him again.

The three of us followed this man about a quarter of a mile when he stopped, pointed to a house, and gestured with his hand for us to follow him in.

"Thank God. We are finally here," I said to the Aussies, as they both said "No shit, mate," at the same time.

We were directed to take our seats in the backyard, which we obliged.

A young boy about the age of nine, and a very old woman about the age of 99 appeared at the back door of the house. The boy, who spoke some English, introduced himself as Youn, and pointed to the old lady saying that this was his grandmother. The man that brought us there was his father, the son of the *very* elderly looking old lady standing in front of us.

"Oh, that's great. Nice to meet you," I said. "We are just here because your father is making us lunch with the fish we all caught today."

Who I am convinced is the oldest looking lady in the entire world said something to the boy in Sri Lankan and he said to us "Just tea here. No lunch."

The Aussies and I looked at each other in disbelief.

"What?" I said to the boy, "We are not eating lunch here?"

"No. My father and I do not live here. You are visiting my grandma for some tea. My father left and is buying vegetables at the store."

So the three of us sat in the backyard, silently drinking tea that none of us wanted due to the fact that it was about 110 degrees outside.

Some time later, after all of our tea was gone and we were all staring at each other, the man came back and said something in Sri Lankan to his son which prompted the boy to say to us "We can go now."

Finally, I thought, *time for lunch*.

We walked only a few steps down the road when the man flagged down a bus, spoke to the driver, then turned to us, gesturing for us to get on the bus.

"I can not get on this bus, my friend," I said, "I have no shoes, no shirt, and I am in a damp bathing suit."

"Yes. You come to our house. You have to," was his response.

And before I knew it, I was half naked on a bus filled to the max with Sri Lankans. And after a very awkward twenty minute bus ride, we finally arrived at the stop for the man's house.

We followed him and his son inside. The 80 pound, nine year-old Sri Lankan boy disappeared into his bedroom only to resurface a minute later with one of his shirts.

"You wear this," he said, handing me his shirt. "But I have no shoes for you to wear. I am very sorry."

Even when you are open to all of the possibilities of what can happen to you when you are traveling around the world, nothing can prepare you for being in a skin tight boys size medium t-shirt, in a strange Sri Lankan village, with an Australian couple you met just hours ago, and inside the home of a local family, none of which speak any English besides the 9-year old son. But here I was.

The boy left, and the three of us were left awkwardly sitting on the living room floor as the man started gutting the fish and his wife began preparing our meal for us.

The hospitality we received from the hosts was noteworthy, even though we could only communicate through the use of smiles and hand gestures.

The food was, indeed, incredible and it was one of the best seafood meals I have ever eaten. There were appetizers, soups, side dishes, and pounds upon pounds of various types of fish. It was a buffet of fresh Sri Lankan seafood.

"Wow, they really went all out for us, huh," I said to my Australian acquaintances.

After we couldn't eat anymore we decided we should thank the couple for their generosity and head home. The awkwardness factor when we were all done eating was through the roof.

But then the man gestured for us to come into his backyard. Once there, he pointed to the roof of his shed.

"Money," the man said. Apparently he knew at least one word in English.

"No. I do not have money," I said. "I am in a bathing suit and your son's shrunken t-shirt."

"Money," he said to the Aussies, a bit more insistent this time.

"No. No money,'" they said.

And we all proceeded to stare at each other, not knowing what to say.

Just then the boy returned home and explained to us that we were here because his father and mother cooked us a meal and in return we would give them money to fix their shed.

We were bamboozled. Was this all a trick to get us to give this guy money? What about all that labor we did this morning? We were told this would be our payment.

"No. That was just to have fun fishing," said the boy.

We just wanted to get the hell out of there at this point. So the Aussies said they will give them money for the three of us and I could pay them when we get back to the beach, seeing as I had no money, no phone, no shoes, and no shirt.

"Fine. Just give him what he wants and let's go," I agreed, pissed.

As we were preparing to leave, the boy said to me "You keep shirt." By this time I forgot I was still wearing the damn thing. I think my torso had become numb from lack of circulation due to how tight the shirt was on me.

I said "No way, this is yours. I have plenty of shirts at the hotel." But the boy insisted.

The shirt was tighter than a wetsuit top and so small that my belly button was uncovered. But at that point I don't think I was going to be able to get out of it without having it cut from my body, so I agreed to wear it on the bus ride home.

So around 4:00 p.m. the bus came to pick us up. It was filled with workers returning home from their long work day. I do not speak Sri Lankan, but I didn't need to in order to understand what all the whispers were about. A shoeless white man wearing a nine-year-old's t-shirt on a Sri Lankan bus kind of speaks for itself. I was half expecting people to start handing me money because they thought I was homeless.

To top off this day from hell, it started downpouring on our way home. And when I returned to my hotel, soaked from head to toe from the rain, I was locked out of my room (Jens and Joss just assumed I was murdered at this point, so they went on an excursion.) I had no phone, no wallet, and no book to read.

Until I excitedly remembered I left my copy of my favorite book, *The Catcher in the Rye* in the hammock.

The hammock outside… in the pouring rain… ruined. Sometimes, not even paradise is all it is cracked up to be.

14. Sri Lanka Moderate Budget Bloody Tea Time

Despite its size, Sri Lanka is the world's fourth largest tea producing country, and the third largest exporter of tea. Lipton tea was founded in Sri Lanka back in 1890 when Sir Thomas Lipton purchased 5,500 acres of the Dambatenne Tea Plantation and began exporting the tea directly to his shops in the UK. Each year tea production and distribution contributes to billions of dollars for Sri Lanka, and is responsible for over a million jobs in the tiny island nation.

Naturally, we needed to see what all the fuss was about, so Joss and I (Swiss Jens parted ways with us to explore Eastern Sri Lanka) traveled from the beautiful white sand beaches of Tangalle to the center of the country to Nawalapitiya to spend some time on a tea plantation in the middle of the Sri Lankan jungle.

The stark contrast between Tangalle and Nawalapitiya is like falling asleep on an overwater beach hut in the Maldives and waking up in a treehouse in the Amazon. It is vast.

The first thing I did after we arrived at our tea cottage resort via a harrowing journey to the top of a mountain in the middle of the jungle was Google "Was Jurassic Park filmed in Nawalapitiya" because I was convinced I was going to see dinosaurs casually strolling through our backyard. It turns out it wasn't filmed there, but I clearly wasn't the first person to Google that because all I had to type into the search bar was *was* "Jurassic Park filmed in N" and Google suggested that I wanted to finish my thought with Nawalapitiya, which can not be a mere coincidence.

The Nawalapitiya Tea Cottage sits perched 2750 feet above sea level in the central highlands on the Greenwood Estate. Home to over 200 acres of lush green tea plantation, it is the perfect spot to explore what all this Sri Lankan tea buzz is all about.

The owners of the resort set up an appointment for Joss and I to take a tour of the tea factory on site and enjoy samples of various teas that are grown and produced on the plantation.

To get to the factory we needed to follow a zig-zagging trail that led its way through the plantations. It was a small dirt road that stretched from our cottage all the way to the factory. Even without the trail we would have been able to follow the scent, as we were like sniffer dogs confirming we were getting closer and closer to the factory with each increasingly fragrant whiff of fresh tea leaves.

We were greeted at the factory by our tour guide, Kasun, who was a young man in his twenties and had more knowledge about tea than I do about every other general knowledge topic combined. His passion for the beverage held my pathetic attention span for about 90 seconds before I started scanning the facility for the tea tasting station, which was really all I cared about.

When someone is passionate about something, they love nothing more than to share every detail of their knowledge with anyone that will listen. So during a seemingly never-ending tour through the factory and intricate details about each and every step of the tea-making process, Kasun finally led us to the tea tasting room. You can only feign interest in something you don't really give a shit about for so long before your cover is blown, and from the looks on mine and Joss's face, Kasun could tell we had reached our tea-making knowledge boiling point.

Like the best part of any brewery or vineyard tour, it was now time for the part everyone was waiting for, the tasting.

Kasun handed us over to the tea tasting room employees and they poured us our first cup of tea, explaining in great detail about the particular leaf used, the process, and the history behind the specific vintage.

Here we go again, I thought to myself.

Can't they just pour the damn tea and shut up about it already, I whispered to Joss, who nodded in agreement as he was blowing on his scorching hot tea.

All eyes were on us while we sipped our tea as every employee was anxiously awaiting for our sign of approval. "Oh wow!" I exclaimed, in my most overly dramatic tone, as if it was the best thing I have ever tasted in my life. "This is amazing," I said, because I couldn't think of anything else to say.

This process continued until we had both drunk five cups of different teas, each supposedly more "special" and more expensive than the last. Knowing this, I became even more dramatic with my review of each cup. Regardless if I liked a cup more than the last, I would say something like "This cup is *definitely* better than the last one," to which the employee would say something along the lines of "Oh yes, well of course, that's because the process of making *this* particular tea is *blah blah blah blah*" and then I would stop listening and zone out until a new cup of tea was in front of me.

When they were finally done giving us more tea than I have ever hoped to drink in my life, we thanked them for their hospitality, tipped them generously, and began the trek back to our cottage, thankful we did not have to drink another cup, or hear the word "tea" for a very long time.

We were still in sight of the factory when the Sri Lankan skies exploded and what I peg to be the heaviest rain storm in recorded history came thundering down upon us. It took us about twenty minutes to walk from our resort to the factory, so for a second we considered going back into the factory and asking Kasun for a ride back to our cottage in the car, but the potential of having to listen to more tea talk seemed more harrowing than the possibility of dying in a Sri Lankan monsoon, so we carried on.

As we were being pelted with water balloon-sized raindrops our walk slowly turned into a jog, then a full on sprint, wincing with pain, yet laughing about our decision to endure physical torture rather than the mental anguish of hearing any more about tea production.

Then, just as quickly as it began, it ended, and the heat from the midday Sri Lankan sun dried us up, and by the time we reached the cottage, it was like nothing happened.

We returned back to the cottage hotel just in time for Game 3 of the World Series, featuring my team, the Boston Red Sox. Unfortunately for me, there was a inconsequential Sri Lankan local cricket tournament going on at the same time, and the employees were quite jazzed about watching it on the only TV in the lounge area.

Amazingly, despite Nawalapitiya's unsurprisingly awful WiFi, I was able to get score updates on my computer. The only problem being that I had to keep refreshing my screen to receive any updates. As luck would have it, the game ended up being the longest running World Series game of all time... 18 innings. For hours and hours I refreshed my computer screen a few times a minute… just to "watch" them lose the damn game.

When the game ended, I returned to my room to have a quick shower before dinner. I was halfway to my room when I realized one of my feet was slipping and sliding on my sandal.

When I looked down to see what the hell was going on, I saw that my foot looked like it had been butchered. There was blood everywhere and looking back I saw a trail from where I exited the lounge area to where I was standing.

There was no pain, so I was puzzled as to what the hell was going on. I poured the contents of my water bottle on my foot and inspected it for cuts. I found nothing.

Where is all this blood coming from? I said to myself, perplexed.

After further inspection of my foot, I discovered that the source of this bloodbath was coming from between two of my toes. The blood was not coming out like it does with a gash or a deep cut, instead it was almost seeping out, at a rapid pace, the way water would ooze out of a compressed sponge.

An employee came running to me once he saw the trail of blood leading to me flailing around on the ground analyzing my toes. He brought me a solution to clean my foot and a box of bandaids, which were completely useless for the amount of blood coming from me. So he brought me a bandage and wrapped my foot up more securely than the Egyptians wrapped King Tut in his mummification robes.

I hobbled back to the lobby where Joss was oblivious to anything that was happening because he was watching a soccer game. The Apocalypse could be happening, and a British lad would still not know something was amiss if their favorite soccer club is playing.

"What the hell happened to you?," he asked. Which is not the first, nor the last time he has needed to ask me that question.

"I have absolutely no idea," I said, "I was walking to our room, looked down because I was slipping all over the damn place, and saw that my foot was covered in blood."

"Maybe you cut in while we were running home in the monsoon and you didn't feel it because we were already in such pain from the pelting rain," Joss proposed.

"Hmm. That is a shockingly clever suggestion," I replied, "You're probably right."

So that is what we chalked it up to; I sliced my foot running home from a tea factory in a Sri Lankan monsoon. Mystery solved.

Until…

I saw a trail of blood coming from the table to the other side of the outdoor lounge. The side of the lounge that I had never been to. *How the hell is that possible,* I thought. Why would there be a trail of blood, if I never walked over there?

So I followed the trail of blood to the corner of the lounge, hopping on my good foot the entire way. And there, at the end of the trail, was a gigantic blood sucking leech the size of my fist. It looked like a leech you would see in a horror movie and say "Yeah right, like a leech could ever be that big."

I called over the employees and they came running over. "THIS is why I was bleeding?," I cried, "You have these things here? What is it so gigantic?"

"Oh yes, sir. When it rains so hard, the leeches love it very much.
You should always check for leeches in your shoes around here when it rains," said the worker.

Now you tell me, I thought. Probably out loud.

"This is a very big leech. You have very nice blood."

This leech was sucking my blood from my foot for the entire seven hour baseball game… the longest post season baseball game of all time. The leech feasted until he had his full, and I was so busy refreshing the damn 18-inning World Series game that I didn't realize a leech was sucking the life out of me.

After all the commotion ceased and everyone settled down (after I stopped screaming like a little girl) the server in the lounge came over to my table to see if I was still traumatized, and to see if the bleeding stopped. He apologized for the unfortunate incident, as if it was his fault. He even brought with him a special gift for me, as a sign of good gesture.

A hot, steaming pot of their special signature tea.

15. Sri Lanka Luxury Budget Safari Slap

Beaches… tea… wildlife; the Sri Lankan adventure trifecta.

With the first two experiences successfully checked off our list, it was time to tackle the plethora of Sri Lankan wildlife. On a luxury budget with no need for restraint on costs, Joss and I decided to book our very own Steve Irwin and take a safari adventure through Yala National Park, Sri Lanka's most famous wildlife park in Hambantota, Sri Lanka.

As with most things travel related, when taking a safari to search for wildlife, it is imperative that you get there early. Like, why-did-I-even-bother-going-to-sleep, early.

It is the time when the animals start stirring about and begin their daily routine of, well… chilling out, maybe going for a little walk, napping and most importantly, killing each other.

So our safari guide, Adesh, picked us up from our resort in Tissamaharama, Sri Lanka at the stomach-turning time of 5:00 a.m..

"This better be worth it," took the place of "Good morning," when Joss and I stumbled towards the door and made our way onto the safari van waiting outside our resort, already filled with our safari companions. An Australian couple by the names of Brian and Charlotte, and two male travel buddies from New Zealand, both by the name of Alex, would be spending the day with us, as we set off on the 30 minute journey to Yala National Park.

Needless to say the banter was kept to a minimum as the last thing any backpacker wants to see is a clock that says 5:00 a.m.. The only talking that took place was when I realized I did not have any money on me to pay my admission to the park and had to try and convey the message to Adesh that he needed to stop at an ATM so I could get cash, which I am sure prompted all twelve eyes that were on the van besides mine to roll into the back of their heads. Not a good first impression to the strangers I would be spending the day with.

When we reached the park we were the fifth vehicle in line for when the gates opened. We each paid our admission, readied our cameras, and made sure to apply a generous amount of both sunscreen and bug spray on our bodies. We were lectured by Adesh that he would do the absolute very best that he could to spot all the most popular animals in the park, including giraffes, elephants, and possibly even the much sought after, leopard.

This was, however, a safari, and nothing was guaranteed. I have been fortunate enough to have been on a few African safaris before, some were massive hits, others were disappointing misses. It is a risk you are willing to take when you go on any safari.

He reminded us that the tour company is not responsible if we get eaten by a lion, stepped on by an elephant, bit by a poisonous snake, etc. He basically told us he was taking us on a boring ride through the jungle and then we were probably going to die.

With all the talk of logistics out of the way, the gates opened at six on the dot, and we entered the animal kingdom.

There were four vans ahead of us and three vans behind us; for a total of eight vehicles. Each van was filled with tourists adorning their best safari hats, cameras strapped tight around their necks, and smiles from ear to ear. People of all ages from little kids to the elderly were anxiously awaiting getting a first hand look at animals they have waited their whole lives to see.

All eyes were peeled into the jungle. Everyone was competing to be the first to be able to say "Look a giraffe!" or "I see an elephant!" or "Holy shit! A leopard!" and win the award for best amateur safari guide. You could cut the tension with a Sri Lankan machete.

We reached the far end of the park and saw exactly zero animals that we would not normally see walking the streets of Sri Lanka. Round number one of the safari was an epic failure. But spirits were still high, after all, we would be in the van for five hours. Surely the animals would emerge at some point.

As the vans began to turn around all of the safari goers would wave to each other, exchange smiles and greet each other with "Hellos," and other pleasantries.

"The animals should wake up soon," insisted Adesh. We could tell he was starting to feel bad about the lack of excitement so far.
"No worries, man. We have all day," we all responded, hoping to take the pressure off the poor man who had no control of the wild life.

The next couple hours were spent driving back and forth through the same routes and passing the same vans. Each time we passed a van of safari-goers we would notice their faces becoming more and more bleak. It was hot as hell, a very bumpy and uncomfortable ride, and we saw nothing noteworthy at all.

Eventually people stopped waving and smiling when they passed us. We could tell with every passing moment these people were growing more and more miserable. We, ourselves, were bored to tears and tired of searching for animals that may or may not ever appear.

So we decided to spice things up a bit and play a game. Every time we passed another vehicle we would all pretend we were laughing, high-fiving and having the time of our lives. We would loudly yell to each other things like "I think the third leopard we saw was way more beautiful than the first two we saw!" or "Guys, can you believe that elephant had her baby right in front of us? Twins!"

The looks of jealousy and envy from the other van's passengers were well worth the price of the admission to the park.

Our guide, since the safari began, would point out things like birds and deer to us. I swear every time he saw a bird he would stop the car and expect us to take a picture of it. You never realize just how everywhere birds are until you have to stop and look at it every time you see one.

Eventually one of the Alex's said "Hey guys, does anyone give a shit about these birds? Cause I don't, mates," to which we all replied with things like "Nope, not in the slightest," or "I couldn't care less about them," or "I fucking hate birds," (that was mine.)

So very kindly, Alex yelled to the tour guide "Hey Adesh, not to be a jerk or anything, but none of us could give a shit less about these birds, mate" and in that moment Alex #1 became one of my favorite people of all time.

Suddenly, Adesh's walkie talkie went off. He apparently got word from another safari guide that an elephant was roaming around on the other side of the park. He put the pedal to the metal and our slow ride through the jungle turned into a hair raising race against the clock. Our heads were smashing against the top of the van as we were all holding on for dear life.

When we arrived at the supposed scene of the elephant sighting the only sign that it had been there was the fresh smell of dung and the massive droppings it left behind. But no elephant in sight.

How the hell do you lose an elephant? I wondered to myself, but decided not to say it out loud because I felt bad for Adesh.

"How the fuck do you lose an elephant, mate?" yelled Alex, unapologetically from the back.

"He must have went back into the jungle," Adesh said sadly.

"It's OK, Adesh, it's not your fault, buddy, you tried," I said for about the 90th time in three hours.

It was approaching the seventh layer of hell heat, and I was bored out of my mind. So I mentioned that maybe we would all have more fun if we left the park and had Adesh take us sightseeing around the area, perhaps grabbing some lunch along the way.

I became an instant hero as everyone yelled "YES. Please!"

So we told Adesh how fantastic of a job he did and that we were all set driving around the park. We asked him to bring us to local spots that were off the beaten path that he recommended.

"Are you sure?" Adesh asked, "I feel sorry that you did not see much."

"YES. WE ARE SURE," we all shouted back in unison, all of our different accents blending into one voice.

So we took one final look around the park and exited the gates. Waving goodbye to all the unfortunate passengers that were stuck driving around in the excruciating heat for another few hours.

We took a right out of the park, drove about one kilometer down the road and nearly smashed into the ass of a gigantic elephant.

"AN ELEPHANT! AN ELEPHANT!" screamed Adesh, as if it was the first time this Sri Lankan man that probably has an elephant in his backyard had ever seen an elephant.

He was so excited that he was finally able to show us an actual animal.

He did a six point turn so we could get the best angle to get photos of the massive elephant that was casually strolling along the road, stopping every few feet to eat the bananas that Adesh threw from the van.

We all took approximately 40 selfies each with the elephant in the background.

But then I decided that a selfie from the van wasn't enough. I wanted to get closer. I asked if I could get out of the van and Adesh said "Yes, but be very careful. They do not like people around them when they are eating their bananas."

"I'll be fine," I uttered. It will be worth the risk for the epic photo.

So I got out, ran right up to the elephant as Adesh snapped photos of me and the elephant's ass. They were decent photos that I should have been more than happy with.

But after inspecting the set of photos, I said "Hold on, a few more. I can look way better than that."

So I went back to pose with the elephant that was occupied with his bananas. I was so busy trying to perfect the exact pose that I wanted that I didn't notice the 12,000 pound animal lift his hind leg and try to kick me away from his bananas.

"WHOA! Watch out Ryan!" yelled the entire van.

I looked back just in time to see the elephant's leg return to the ground.

"Holy shit! He tried to kick me!" I yelled back to the van, laughing at the close encounter.

"Did you get the pic---" I began to yell back at the van, just as the elephant's massive tail swung towards me and smacked me right in the face.

It struck with such force that it knocked the wind out of me for a brief moment.

I hobbled back to the van filled with six relative strangers that were in fits of laughter.

With a red imprint of an elephant's tail on my already swollen face I said "Adesh, let's get out of here, NOW!" in the most aggressive, yet polite way I know how.

With my face busted, my foot wrapped in bandages from a blood sucking leech, and my ego bruised from being swindled into working as a fisherman for free, it was time to say goodbye to Joss, Jens, and the incredible country of Sri Lanka and try for some better luck in the beautiful Asian nation of Thailand.

16. Thailand - Low Budget Fire in the Sky

Each year thousands of travelers make their way to northern Thailand to witness the Loi Krathong festival held during the full moon in November. The festival is a staple on many traveler's bucket lists, and it just so happens to have been taking place when I arrived in Chiang Mai, Thailand.

Loi Krathong could literally be translated as "to float a basket," and refers to the tradition of locals floating *krathong,* or a buoyant, decorated basket, down the river in the hopes of paying respect to the water spirits. The lit candles floating down the river signify the transition from darkness to a brighter future.

In Chiang Mai, Thailand, however, the tradition of lighting gigantic paper lanterns with a candle and floating them into the sky, has overtaken the basket floating ritual as one of the most picturesque festival activities in the entire world.

In addition to the floating baskets and flying lanterns, Chiang Mai also hosts a myriad of activities, parades, and firework displays in order to commemorate the celebration.

Besides the positive vibes, lively atmosphere, and stunning beauty of the festival, perhaps the best part may be how easy on your wallet the Loi Krathong Festival is. All the events are free to attend, purchasing baskets will cost about $3 USD and buying your own lanterns to float up into the sky to join the army of other lanterns will only cost about $2 USD.

So my new travel companions and I, Marc, a muscular phenomenon from Barcelona with the body fat index of about one percent, Austin, a laid back, surfer dude from Seattle with a set of locks that would make Fabio jealous, and Gaggan from Copenhagen, with a social ability and sense of humor that is, quite frankly, a threat to my own personal strengths, departed for the Loi Krathong Festival, ready to embrace everything the celebration has to offer.

With options for delicious pad thai, banana pancakes, and Chang beers that are so cheap they are basically free, food vendors litter the streets, each stand offering an even more tempting option, for an even cheaper price. People of all ages, ethnicities and backgrounds gather to celebrate the yearly tradition.

As the crowd started to get more and more dense people began bumping into each other due to the fact that our eyes were directed towards the sky lit up with bright orange lanterns rather than focusing on where we were walking.

The deeper we got into the madness of the crowd, the more chaotic the atmosphere became. Spectators would stop in the middle of the sea of people, deciding that would be their prime spot to launch their four foot paper lantern after setting it ablaze. What could go wrong?

In the United States there would be dozens of laws and rules about where and when you can light off your hazardous ball of flames and attempt to release it into the sky. In Thailand, however, there are no such rules. Not only are lanterns mishandled by thousands of virgin firestarters, but more frightening, is the amount of fireworks being lit off by amateurs.

We saw more fireworks malfunctioning on the ground than in the sky, only to hear a roar of laughter coming from the crowd rather than screams of safety concerns.

"This would never be allowed in America," Austin and I said to each other more times than I can count.

When you see pictures of the festival online, the beautifully lit lanterns illuminating the sky seem like tiny dots the size of a soccer ball. In reality they are massive objects that even four grown men had just enough control over to be able to properly work them.

Everywhere you looked there were lanterns catching on fire before they were even released, or getting caught in a gust of wind and crashing down among the crowd. It was raining fireballs, and nobody besides us seemed to be concerned one would fall out of the sky and engulf us.

When we finally made our way to a spot that looked like there was an appropriate amount of space for us to light off our lanterns, we each took turns igniting ours while the other three aided in holding the paper deathtraps so we could all successfully release our lanterns (and subsequent wishes for the year ahead) into the sky.

As each of us let go of our lanterns we would all follow it until it was impossible to decipher ours from the thousands of other blazes, staring longingly, and sharing our gratitude to be able to be a part of transforming the dark sky into a bright orange sea of fire.

Many other festival goers, however, were unable to find the same success as the four of us. Some lanterns may have never left the ground, but others would crash into each other, sending both tumbling to the crowd standing below. And others, looking promising at first, would crash into the branches of surrounding trees, thus igniting the paper lantern, as well as the branches of the innocent trees.

Many people, clearly impressed by our lantern launching abilities, asked for our help with releasing their lanterns into the sky so they could have their wish for the year heard by the gods. Each of us took turns helping as many groups as we could.

Just as we all had agreed that we reached our quota of lantern launching, we headed off to make our way to our favorite Chiang Mai watering hole and celebrate our accomplishments.

But we were stopped by an older man, traveling by himself to the festival all the way from Canada, claiming it has always been a dream of his to attend the festival and light off his very own lantern into the Chiang Mai sky.

"Of course, we would be more than happy to help you," we all replied.

We assumed our positions; I spread out the paper lantern from the bottom while Marc, being the tallest, held the lantern high in the air, and Austin assisted the man with the fire from below, all with the hope of helping this man see his dream become a reality. Gaggan took the man's phone to make sure he had this special moment on film.

The man's face lit up brighter than the orange sky as he saw his lantern expand and swell to take-off size. He was yelling "Are you filming, are you filming?" repeatedly to make sure Gaggan was ready to capture the moment.

"Yes. It's filming!" Gaggan assured the man as each of us gently released the lantern one by one and gave the Canadian man all the control over his inflated lantern.

"When do I release it? Is it ready? Will it work if I let go now?" he yelled.

"Yeah, man, you're good to go! Let it launch!" I yelled.

"OK... here I go... three... two... one..." shouted the man about to fulfill his lifelong dream.

We all cheered him on as he let go of his lantern and it began drifting into the sky. But like a bat out of hell, seconds after the man released his lantern another lantern came plummeting out of the sky, colliding with his lantern and sending both of them crashing to the ground; essentially shattering all of the man's hopes and dreams.

We stared at him. He stared at us. And before we could express our apologies for assuring him he could let go of his lantern, he yells, "It is ok! I bought two!" and whips out another folded lantern from his oversized handbag.

"Awesome! Good thinking man!" we yelled, relieved that he would have another chance of seeing his dream become a reality.

So we resumed our positions and began helping the man with his second lantern, all along reassuring the man that he was bound to be successful with this one.

His excitement reappeared as the lantern was lit and again, he was ready for takeoff.

"OK. Can I release it now?" he asked us.

After scanning the area for anything that could prohibit this man's lantern from a successful launch, we confirmed that he was in the clear and ready to release.

Gaggan fulfilled his role again as cameraman, and the countdown began.

"Three… two… one…" the man dramatically yelled again.

He released his lantern only after looking around the area and making sure it wasn't going to meet the same fate as his first lantern. Clearly he lost all trust in the four of us.

He let go only when he was convinced there were no other lanterns around to crash into his, and it began to float towards the sky.

And just as he began yelling "I did it!, It worked!" a huge gust of wind came out of nowhere and sent his lantern at mach ten speed directly into a tree.

The man with the shittiest luck in all of Thailand watched the lantern in horror as it caught on fire and plummeted out of the tree and onto the ground. We watched his face in disbelief as his hopes and dreams crashed harder than his ill-fated lanterns.

We again apologized as if it was our fault mother nature reared her ugly head at the most inopportune of times, and slowly walked away from the man one at a time, wishing him the best of luck in finding another lantern along with better success.

A few hours later, as we were sitting in our Chiang Mai bar that we frequented every night, the man came running in and screaming "I did it! I did it!" and bought us all beers for all of our help.

It turns out he bought a third lantern basically on the black market of Thailand and I am pretty sure he willingly offered his firstborn male child for it. He went into the streets and launched the lantern all on his own.

This time, however, he had no photographic evidence of his success. Instead, only the memory of following his very own lantern into the Chiang Mai sky, and celebrating by drinking Chang beers and shots of Mekhong whiskey with four strangers from all over the world until the wee hours of the morning.

We may not be the best at assisting strangers in need, but we are absolute legends when it comes to properly celebrating their accomplishments.

17. Thailand
Moderate Budget
The Life of Pai

No matter where I am or who I meet, the question most often asked by people that hear about my venture around the world is "What was your favorite place?"

While it is certainly possible to consider a great number of destinations as my favorite place in the world, the reply that always jumps from my lips before I can think about the answer is Pai, Thailand.

Pai, Thailand, relatively unknown to most Westerners (unless you are an avid backpacker), is a small town located in northwestern Thailand, about 90 miles northwest of Chiang Mai and a stone's throw from the Myanmar border.

The follow up question, of course, is always "What about it makes it your favorite place?"

My response is simple: "Everything."

For starters, the weather is exceptional, albeit a little too hot sometimes, which can quickly be resolved by taking a swim in one of their many watering holes.

Additionally, the scenery is akin to something you would see in the Garden of Eden. Stunning waterfalls, mind-blowing canyons, and pristine hiking trails will make you wonder why anyone would live anywhere besides this small Thai town.

But by far and away the most magical thing about Pai is the people. The locals, many of whom are expats that visited the town and quite simply could not bear to leave (often referred to as the "Pai Effect"), are some of the most inviting, welcoming, and kind-hearted people I have met in my entire life. They treat foreigners like family instantly, and without discrimination.

Even more fascinating is that the positivity and friendliness of the locals transmits itself directly to everyone that steps foot into the town. Everyone is smiling. Everyone is greeting each other. In Pai, Thailand there is no such thing as a stranger.

If you are sitting by yourself at a bar or restaurant, you will be bombarded with requests from other travelers to sit with them, enjoy some drinks, or play some games. More than likely they will *insist* you sit with them, *insist* you play games with them, and *insist* they pay for whatever drink you want. You don't really have a choice. Then, inevitably, you find yourself doing the same thing to others. It's basically a hippy's version of the circle of life.

It is like the real life version of *Mr. Roger's Neighborhood*. They might as well be playing the "Won't You Be My Neighbor" song on a loudspeaker and blaring it throughout the town.

I would not be surprised to see a breaking news alert a few years from now that says Pai, Thailand is under scrutiny for filtering laughing gas through their air stream. That would maybe explain why everyone is so damn happy and smiley all the time.

Plus, an added bonus… Long Island Iced Teas are like a dollar. So there's that.

So when my traveling compadres I met in Chiang Mai, Marc (the muscular one), Austin (the cool one), and Gaggan (the funny one) traveled to Pai, we were in our glory.

Since everything is so cheap in Pai, the times that we were not busy smiling at strangers, hugging locals, and in a state of totally natural euphoric bliss, we rented mopeds to experience some of the marvels of Pai; other than the people.

When I say "We" rented mopeds, I really mean "The three of them" rented mopeds and I straddled Marc's back all day, holding on for dear life as he fearlessly blazed through the hillside.

Of course as we passed other travelers coming from the opposite direction, everyone was frantically waving at each other as if we were best friends that hadn't seen each other in way too long.

Our first stop was one of the many waterfalls in Pai, the Pam Bok. After parking our bikes and basically telling random strangers that just happened to be standing in the parking lot that we loved them, we hiked to a gorgeous waterfall hidden in the mountains. If you look up serenity in the dictionary, you will see a picture of Pam Bok.

Some people were effortlessly floating on their backs, letting their bodies whisk away to a state of pure relaxation.

Some people were having a picnic with a group of friends (presumably a group of strangers they just met minutes prior and are now in each other's wills) and smiling ear to ear.

And some were casually walking in the sea of picture perfect crystal clear water, inching closer and closer to the waterfall, until, finally, they were standing underneath it, posing for a legendary Instagram pic for the ages.

We spent the day jumping off cliffs, taking turns being pelted with the powerful waterfall, making new friends (as if we needed anymore in Pai) and embracing the pure beauty surrounding us.

Before sundown the entire waterfall crew, like *literally* everyone that was at the waterfall, decided to visit Pai Canyon, which is well known to be one of the most beautiful places in Thailand, if not the world, to watch the sunset.

I do have to admit, however, that the Pai Canyon ridges you must walk along to get your coveted front row seats for the sunset are harrowing, especially if you are anything like me and have an irrational, paralyzing fear of heights.

But the reward far outweighs the risk, as the sun setting over the Pai Canyon is as close to life-changing as a sunset can be.

Hundreds of people gather to sit on the sandy floor at the peak of Pai Canyon and become tranquilized by its beauty.

There are no signs saying "Silence Please" or "Quiet Area," but naturally everyone in the audience sits motionless as the sun sets for the evening. Hundreds of strangers sitting within inches of each other fall into complete silence and wait to watch the sun retire for the day.

In fact, when someone from our crew started whispering something to another member, we would all jokingly respond with a "Ssshhhh" and hold our index finger to our lips the way a librarian would to chatty children in the library.

For four days Gaggan, Marc, Austin and I would joke that nobody has ever gotten into an argument in Pai, Thailand. Nobody has ever been angry in Pai Thailand. And nobody has ever not smiled while wandering the peaceful, laid back streets of Pai, Thailand.

Just as the sun disappeared behind the mountains we gathered up our belongings and began the trek back over the ridges to begin our descent down the canyon.

But just as we were crossing the death-defying ridges we heard music playing from a couple's phone. They were sitting with their legs dangling over the canyon and enjoying the sunset with some reggae music (obviously.)

We looked at each other almost frightened, as if they were breaking the first cardinal rule of watching sunsets in the Pai Canyon.

About 50 yards down from the rule-breaking music lovers were two girls, also with their legs dangling over the canyon and trying to peacefully enjoy the final moments of the epic sunset.

As we walked by, one of the girls started yelling at the top of her lungs to the couple playing the music.

"HEY! HEY YOU! YOU WITH THE MUSIC PLAYING!" one of the girls screamed. She was trying desperately to get the "rule-breaker's" attention, but due to the fact that the music was playing from their phone so loud, the couple were completely oblivious to the girl's hollers.

Our group stopped dead in our tracks, flabbergasted that we were about to witness an angry conflict in Pai. To avoid any such confrontation and to keep the peace, I walked back over to the couple and calmly told them that there were two girls down the cliff that were screaming at them.

The hippy couple calmly turned down the music, thanked me for getting their attention and looked at the girl that was still screaming her head off.

"YOU TWO DOWN THERE! IS THAT YOU PLAYING MUSIC RIGHT NOW?" the girl, who looked relieved to finally be able to relay her message to the couple yelled.

The couple turned back to me and stared confused, as I shrugged my shoulders as if to say "I have no idea who these angry girls are, I am just an innocent bystander trying to keep the peace in Pai."

"YES. SORRY. IT IS OUR MUSIC!" the male hippy yelled back to the frantic girl.

"I FUCKING LOVE IT, DUDE!!!!" screamed the girl as her and her friend gave a thumbs up to the hippy couple.

The hippy couple flashed the peace sign back to the girls, yelled "RIGHT ON!" and turned up their Bob Marley even louder, and continued staring off into the picture-perfect orange and pink sky of Pai, Thailand; the happiest place on Earth.

18. Thailand – Luxury Budget
Finding Mr. Brightside

Growing up, some people dream of having a big, beautiful house with a white picket fence. Others dream of living on a ranch with nothing but acres of land engulfing them. And of course many even dream of living in an Italian villa surrounded by the Mediterranean Sea.

Not me.

My dream accommodations for as long as I can remember; living at Melrose Place.

The hit 90's TV show where a rotating group of singles had their own small, yet upscale apartment quarters with a shared inground swimming pool was all I ever wanted.

So when I arrived at my luxury hotel, The Privilege Ezra Beach Resort on the island of Koh Samui, Thailand, I felt like I had died and gone to heaven.

Meeting me for this leg of the venture was fellow wandering nomad American, Ian, who I met a few months prior in Bosnia and Herzegovina. We shared a hostel in Mostar and realized our travel itineraries would enable us to reunite for a few weeks while exploring the Thai Islands.

He was arriving a day after me, so I was flying solo when I walked into the resort that blew Melrose Place out of the water. Located directly on the beach, the resort was exactly what you would expect a modern day version of Melrose Place to look like.

A massive inground swimming pool with a swim-up pool bar was at the center of the resort, with deluxe, posh, modern living quarters surrounding the water.

If there is a world record for the fastest time any human being has ever gone from the check-in desk to sitting on the bar stumps in the pool, I have it clinched.

But even more impressive than that, I think I now own the world record for becoming best friends with three strangers faster than any relationship has ever formed.

Sitting on the lounge chairs outside of their room, three Belgians were staring me down, then staring at each other, then back at me sitting on the pool bar stools. Seeing as it was not even noon yet, they looked at each other and nodded, as if saying "If it isn't too early for him to start drinking, it isn't too early for us to start."

So within minutes the once empty bar stools next to me were filled with my new best friends, Jorn, Zoe and Farah from Antwerp, Belgium.

It has been established already that I can make a new best friend anywhere, be it while lying in a hospital bed or attending a particularly tragic funeral.

But these three friends were different. Despite being from different continents, by the time we finished our first frozen beverages we felt like we had known each other our entire lives.

This is a brief summary of how our conversation went:

0:01 minute into meeting - standard introductions. Names. Where we are from. How long we were traveling for. Where else we have traveled. The boring stuff that many long term travelers dread having to repeat over and over again day after day.

0:03 minutes into meeting - We told each other how happy we were that we were staying at the same place.

0:04 minutes into meeting - We made plans to go on a cruise together the following day.

0:07 minutes into meeting - We bonded over reality tv and music.

0:09 minutes into meeting - We invited each other into our homes in our respective countries.

0:10 minutes into meeting - We repeatedly told each other how much we love each other.

The rest is history.

The Pina Coladas were flowing. And the Chang beers were flowing even harder.

The party was started.

****

We spent hours taking turns going from the ocean to the pool (a.k.a. bar stools) and back again. There was no denying that we were the fun side of the pool and people were beginning to take notice.

In particular, there was a couple sitting in silence at the opposite end of the pool. Every time one of us looked to the boring side of the pool, we saw the male half of the couple eyeing us. It wasn't a judging look, it was more of a look of pure jealousy.

Clearly the guy would have much preferred to be partying with the four of us rather than sitting next to his boring girlfriend.

The girl, however, was staring at us too, but her look was more of a "Look at those four disgusting people drinking so early," look.

So when the judgy girlfriend decided to go for a dip in the ocean, I took it as my opportunity to be the good samaritan that I am, and go to the other end and ask the guy if he wanted to join us on the fun end.

I informed Jorn, Zoe and Farah of my mission, and received their full support.

So I swam to the other end of the pool. And by "Swam" I mean "I kicked my legs and paddled with one arm while holding my Pina Colada high enough in the air to avoid getting pool water in it."

Before I could even introduce myself the guy says to me, "Hey, want a Long Island Iced Tea? It's buy one get one free and I need to get rid of this hangover."

Those were literally the first words this kid ever uttered to me. I suppose *technically* this isn't a case of love at first sight, but more of a case of "Love at first sentence."

"I'd love a Long Island Iced Tea," I said. "And my name is Ryan."

"I'm Luke, cheers mate."

And with that, Luke flagged down the nearest employee, and said "Four Long Island Iced Teas, please."

He then looked back at me and said "You didn't think I was only going to have one, did you? "When I said "It's buy one get one free," I meant "I'll buy one and get one free for myself, and i'll buy you one and get you one for free too.""

And with that… the most epic bromance of all time was born.

"How long are you and your friends traveling for mate?" Luke from England asked as we sipped on our Long Island Iced Teas.

"Oh, I just met them like an hour ago," I told Luke.

"You're messing with me, mate," he said. "You guys look like you are best friends."

"We are," was my response.

****

So I introduced Luke to Jorn, Zoe, and Farah, and we all spent the day laughing, cheersing, hugging, and telling stories. All the while Luke's girlfriend was tanning quietly on the boring side of the pool.

For hours Luke and I were inseparable. At one point we were even having chicken fights against no one. We would just take turns carrying one another on each other's shoulders and walking around the pool saying hello to people.

It was a perfect day in paradise until Luke asked me what my favorite song was. Before I could even answer (because I was busy ordering anyone in sight a round of drinks from the pool bar bartender) my Belgian friends all yelled ""Mr. Brightside" by The Killers!"

Clearly I had mentioned it a few times to them already.

Upon hearing the news Luke jumped on my back and nearly drowned me out of excitement.

"The Killers are my favorite band, mate!" Luke screamed.

"That settles it. We are all going to find a karaoke bar tonight and I am singing "Mr. Brightside,"" I insisted.

Jorn, Zoe and Farah jumped with joy, while Luke and I embraced and finished our drinks.

"Let's all go to our rooms and shower and change and meet back here in a half hour. We will get a cab to the bar section of town. There must be karaoke somewhere," Jorn suggested.

"Brilliant," we all yelled.

So after the longest half hour of my life being separated from my four best friends of all time, I emerged from my room ready to debut my "Mr. Brightside" karaoke abilities to Luke, Jorn, Zoe and Farah (and whatever Luke's girlfriend's name was if she insisted on tagging along.)

As if on cue, the Belgians come out of their room, ready for a night out on the Koh Samui town. We looked around for Luke and there was no sign of him anywhere.

"Umm, excuse me, do you know where Luke is?" I said to his boring girlfriend that probably hated my guts.

"Who knows. He is probably looking for you," she said, kind of jokingly, but mostly scornful.

Moments after she hissed those words I heard a loud "RYANNNNNNNN!"

"Where have you been, mate? I have been looking for you everywhere" a very inebriated Luke uttered to me.

"Umm, I was in my room, literally right behind you, and exactly where I said I was going to be. Why are you still in your bathing suit?" I asked.

"I was scared to go to my room because I didn't want you to leave without me. I am just going like this," said a soaking wet, shirtless Luke.

"Well, I couldn't care any less what you wear," I said, "but the owners of the bar and the taxi man might care," as I was being pulled to the front doors of our hotel by the Belgians, who clearly did not want to have to babysit Luke all night long.

The taxi arrived and Jorn, Zoe, Farah and I got in, while Luke attempted to get in, still soaking wet and trying to convince the taxi driver that it was ok, because he was "with Ryan."

After much deliberation, and convincing, I was forced to say my least favorite sentence I have ever been forced to say… "Luke, I don't think you can come with us."

Luke, devastated, looked around the taxi and saw the rest of the crew nodding in agreement and said, "Can we swim in the pool together again all day tomorrow then?"

As my heart shattered into a million pieces I said "I promise we can Luke," and shut the door knowing full well that I had a cruise booked with Jorn, Zoe, Farah, and my friend Ian, and hoping that he would be too hungover the next day to even think about playing in the pool.

Now that Luke was out of the picture, it was time to focus on the task at hand… finding a karaoke bar.

The taxi dropped us off in the thick of the Koh Samui action. We walked up and down each street, popping our head in each bar, asking where the closest karaoke place was.

We were led on a wild goose chase, and every lead turned out to be a disappointing "No karaoke tonight" response.

So when we passed the busiest bar in the area, which had a live band playing, we decided that we might as well check it out, seeing as we came all the way to this part of town.

We walked in and the lead singer was playing a song by Pearl Jam. "This place will do just fine," I said to my friends.

Then the next song was by Blink 182, yet another of my favorite bands. I was loving life.

The band was not accepting requests, but that didn't stop me from walking up to the lead singer, giving him a high five, telling him I loved the band, and asking them if they knew "Mr. Brightside" by The Killers.

"Yeah we can do that," the lead singer assured me.

"Can I sing it?" I asked the singer.

"You want to sing with me? On stage?" the man responded.

"No. I want you to leave the stage and I want to sing Mr. Brightside with the band."

The lead singer stared at me, looked at his guitar player, who shrugged his shoulders, and then looked back at me and said "Do you know all the words?"

"Don't insult me, of course I know all the words," I said, which made the band burst out laughing.

"OK. Get up here."

The lead singer left the stage, I took the mic, the guitar riff started, and I yelled "This is for you, Luke. Wish you could be here with us!," as the crowd let out a collective "Awe, that's so sweet" probably because they thought that Luke was a loved one that tragically lost his life and is no longer with us. Little did they know that I met Luke only a few hours prior and he was very much alive just a few miles away. He was just very drunk.

After pulling on the heartstrings of the audience, I tore the Koh Samui roof down with the most heartfelt version of Mr. Brightside ever sung.

When we got back to the resort a few hours later, we were informed that the hot tub, which is normally open 24 hours a day, would be closing at midnight because the Princess of Thailand was arriving from a late flight and the hot tub was directly under her suite.

I took a step back and admired the fact that the Princess of Thailand was staying at the same resort we were, just upstairs and a few rooms down from me. In the room *directly* next to Luke's.

"I sure hope Luke doesn't look out the window, see that I am home, and come down and want to party more, we can't disturb the Princess of Thailand," I whispered to my new Belgians friends.

It was the biggest lie I ever told them.

19. Laos - Low Budget In a Barbie World

Many long term travelers create ongoing playlists of songs they hear over the course of their adventure. Upon returning home and listening to the playlist, they are transported back to the time and place of their journey where that specific song left an impression.

Each destination I travel to I typically end up adding two or three songs that will forever remind me of my time in that town or city. Some songs are culturally significant; some even in different languages.

Yet others are songs that either come up in conversation with new friends, or songs that were playing at a bar that got a group of strangers to have a sing-along, or, of course, songs that get the crowds pumped up during a night out at karaoke.

****

Every morning at sunrise in Huay Xai , Laos the monks participate in a morning alms ceremony in which they will receive donations of food prepared by the locals or participating tourists. In return they will pray over and bless the observers.

Neither the monks nor the locals speak during the ritual. Me: attending a ceremony where silence is of paramount importance?

Mistake number one.

But on my first morning in Laos I decided to wake up at the nauseatingly early time of five in the morning in order to witness the ceremony. I was on a low budget, and therefore I was staying at a hostel.

I packed my day bag the night before so as to not wake up my roommates at the ungodly hour. I then drugged myself to sleep with ambien extra early, so when my alarm went off, I popped right out of bed, grabbed my bag, and quietly snuck out of the room, nary waking a sole.

As I was gingerly walking along the dark streets of Huay Xai the silence of the desolate neighborhood was deafening. So I plugged my headphones into my phone, and slowly trotted along to the Venture Twelve playlist that I created on Spotify.

I quietly sang along to the Italian classic "La Canzone del Sole," which was first introduced to me by two Italian girls from Milan I met during my stay at a wine themed hotel in Porto, Portugal.

My relaxing walk became much peppier when "Waka Waka (This Time for Africa)" by Shakira came on. The song, despite being nearly a decade old, is still a radio staple just about everywhere in the world besides the US. To be perfectly honest, I am sure I listened to it twice on my walk to the monk ceremony, because I do not think I am physically capable of listening to that gem only one time.

And finally, just as I approached the monk ceremonies I was wrapping up "Don't Look Back in Anger" by Oasis. This made the list due to the fact that it is my go-to karaoke song to get the crowd pumped up before "Mr. Brightside" and I made exceptional use of it while traveling Eastern Europe.

As I approached the people gathered for the ceremony, I unplugged my headphones, neatly wrapped them up in a perfect little circle, put them in my designated "headphone pocket" of my backpack, (which I'm convinced has an invisible little elf in it whose job it is to tie as many knots in them as possible while I am not using them) and put my phone in my backpack.

I sat down on the sidewalk and prepared to get my inner monk on. I was mentally prepared to be silent, not look the monks in the eye, not touch the monks, and keep my head lower than the monks', which is a show of respect. A lot of things to remember at 6am, right?

As the sun began to rise on the streets of Huay Xai, the orange gowns of the silent monks began to appear one at a time, all in a perfect line, and looking like they were more than ready to bless the shit out of me.

I am a greeter by nature. I love saying "Hello," to anyone that even glances in my direction. It's actually very difficult for me to not say hello to people, or at least give a little head nod and smile as a form of acknowledgement. You should see me walking through Times Square in New York City. From behind I swear it must look like I am having a seizure because my head is bobbing up and down so much; attempting to greet uninterested strangers who are trying to mind their own business.

So anyway, it took every ounce of self control I have to not say "Hello! How are you?" or hug the monks that are not allowed to touch anyone.

But all I did was gently nod my head towards my prayer hands to acknowledge their presence. I swear I haven't looked that holy since my first communion polaroid camera photo shoot back in 1987.

I did notice, however, that my gawky backpack was still attached to my back, so I made the decision to take it off, to avoid looking like I was in a rush to get the hell out of there the second the monks passed me.

So I slid my bag off my shoulders while still silently nodding like an idiot at each monk that passed me by.

Mistake number two...

****

Back in Bosnia and Herzegovina our entire hostel went on a 12 hour tour, visiting historic war sites, swimming in beautiful waterfalls, and hiking to the top of gorgeous mountainside villages.

This experience bonded a group of us to the point that many of us traveled together for weeks on end.

In the days following our Bosnia and Herzegovina tour, we would spend plenty of nights visiting some of the local bars, many of which featured live entertainment.

For some reason or another we kept hearing the classic 1997 song by bubblegum pop Danish-Norwegian band Aqua, "Barbie Girl." During one of the intermissions from live music, two members of the group even gathered on a popular footbridge in Mostar, Bosnia and Herzegovina and did a not-so killer rendition of "Barbie Girl" with one playing the role of Barbie and the other playing the role of Ken. It made me laugh.

Needless to say, "Barbie Girl" was added to the Venture Twelve playlist.

****

    I was sliding my bag off of my shoulders slower than a sloth in order to not make a commotion in front of the meditating monks. I was also trying to not cause too much movement, so I probably looked like Harry Houdini trying to escape a straightjacket. But, I did it. I slid my backpack off and placed it on the ground next to me without so much as a rustle.

    After I let go of the bag I heard two muffled voices having a conversation. I looked behind me to see who was being so rude as to have a conversation at this very moment. I saw nobody behind me.

****

The song "Barbie Girl" begins with a conversation between the most legendary dolls of all time, Ken and Barbie. The voices used to portray the duo are quite possibly the most overdramatic, obnoxious voices ever used in recorded history.

Here is the dialogue…

Ken: "Hiya Barbie."
Barbie: "Hi Ken!"
Ken: "You want to go for a ride?"
Barbie: "Sure Ken!"
Ken: "Jump in!"
(motorcycle engine grinding)

****

    It wasn't until I heard the revving of Ken's engine that I realized where the noise was coming from. It wasn't two rude tourists interrupting the alms giving ceremony. It was Ken and Barbie. On my phone. Zipped up neatly in my backpack.

I swear I could see a dinosaur walking around my backyard and Adam and Eve swimming in my pool and my eyes would not bulge out of my head harder or faster than they did when I realized that "Barbie Girl" was blasting in my bag during the monk's morning alms giving ceremony in Laos.

Of all the songs in quite literally all of the world, this is what happens to be playing next on my phone. I could not think of a more unfortunate song to be playing.

I, of course, went into full on panic mode as the lyrics sprang into life. I didn't want to open the bag and cause more of a disruption, so I simply hugged my bag as tight as I could, hoping to muffle the sound so much that it could not be heard by the completely silent monks or the completely silent locals.

But despite how hard I hugged the bag, I could still hear Ken and Barbie getting their party on. The beginning of the song isn't wildly inappropriate, but it is extraordinarily embarrassing.

Barbie: "I'm a Barbie girl, in a Barbie world. Life in plastic, it's fantastic. You can brush my hair, undress me everywhere. Imagination, life is your creation."

Ken: "Come on Barbie, let's go party."

So I devised a plan. The first part of the song repeats itself twice before an instrumental break. I would hug the ever-loving shit out of my bag until the first section was done, then during the instrumental section, quietly open my bag and shut it off before the first wildly inappropriate verse began.

Mistake number three.

"I'm a Barbie girl, in a Barbie world. Life in plastic, it's fantastic. You can brush my hair, undress me everywhere. Imagination, life is your creation."

There is about four seconds of downtime in the song before the verse kicks in hard. I had one chance at this...

I quickly unzipped by bag, reached my hand in for the phone, couldn't find it, and hastily stood up to walk away as *"I'm a blonde, bimbo girl, in a fantasy world, dress me up, make it tight, I'm your dolly,"* rang through the air even louder due to the fact that my bag was now unzipped and I wasn't squeezing my bag with every ounce of energy I had.

I ran away on the tips of my toes more gingerly and swiftly than the Pink Panther and dove down the first sidestreet I saw, my face redder than Superman's cape and my dignity nonexistent.

With my head in my hands, I realized that there was clearly only one solution to this; I must walk into the Mekong River and drown myself.

After much debate I decided there may be a second, less permanent solution. I now must hire a Michelin Star chef, take a trip back to Laos, have the chef prepare a five star meal for 1,000 monks, and have someone responsible deliver said meals to the generous monks during the alms giving ceremony at sunrise as I stay in bed until noon.

Where I belong.

20. Laos - Moderate Budget
The Slow (Love) Boat

Without a doubt, one of the most epic things to do when you are in Laos is to take the slow boat down the Mekong River. The journey begins on the Thailand/Laos border and takes two days (with an overnight stay at a guesthouse along the way) to arrive at the capital of Laos, Luang Prabang. So for about 15 hours you slowly drift down the Mekong River, continuously surrounded by the breathtaking scenery and engulfed by the stunning beauty of Laos.

Due to a lack of entertainment options, however, the boredom may get to you. There are no TV's, there is no wi-fi, and there is no shuffleboard or coordinated activities to help you to pass the time. Sure, you could stick your nose in a book for a few hours, but then you would be doing yourself a disservice by not taking in all of the beauty surrounding you in Laos, essentially wasting an experience that you may never get the opportunity to do again.

But you know what the slow boat does have… a makeshift bar, as well as other bored-out- of-their-mind passengers from across the globe. If you take 100 strangers from all over the world, stick them on a very slow boat drifting down the Mekong River over the course of two days, and supply them with $1.50 16oz. beers, suddenly that slow boat doesn't seem so slow anymore. And just like that, you will be supplied with all of the entertainment you will need to make your journey more memorable than a 10-night Royal Caribbean cruise.

As the passengers began boarding the boat and choosing their seats for the journey, it became obvious that people were trying to silently size each other up to see who would be the best passengers to sit next to. This is a decision that must be taken very seriously. If you get stuck next to neighbors that are boring, dull or snoozes, your slow boat journey could be disastrous.

If, however, you choose to sit next to passengers that are fun, energetic, and ready to turn the slow boat into the love boat, you are in for the two day journey of a lifetime.

So when my traveling companion, Marc and I boarded the boat and saw it nearly empty, I started to panic a bit. Sure I could choose the most comfortable seat, in the best location on the boat, but what about my neighbors? What if I choose my seat and then a bunch of snoozefests surrounded me, essentially ruining my good time?

So I did what any logical person would do and went up to the bar, ordered five gigantic BeerLao beers, and returned to my seat. I cracked open the first of the beers, and placed it, and all four remaining beers on the communal table in front of me.

My strategy was that if someone was getting on the slow boat and had the intention of being boring, reading, or sleeping, they would not want to sit next to a loud American guy that has 96 ounces of beer in front of him and they would carry on to another section of the boat.

In contrast, if someone was getting onto the slow boat in hopes that it would turn into some sort of Laotian booze cruise, they would see me with the beers ready to go, plop their asses down right next to be, and before the boat left the dock, we would be the very best of friends.

My plan, as usual, worked like a charm.

The first people that boarded the boat after I returned to my seat took one look at me and quickly looked away, as if they were trying not to get caught judging me. They briskly kept walking, making their way as far along to the back of the boat as possible. Clearly, they wanted nothing to do with having any fun whatsoever.

But the next passenger, Jess, a lively, energetic, bubbly solo passenger from Barcelona, loudly exclaimed "I *know where I am sitting*," in a thick Spanish accent after seeing my BeerLaos. We high fived before introducing ourselves and without so much as another word, I slid a beer over to her, she cracked it open, we clinked cans and said "Tham keo" (cheers in Laotian.) We didn't know, but this was the first moment of what would turn into nearly three weeks of traveling through Laos together.

Suddenly, the traveling twosome of Marc and I turned into a threesome and the epic Laos group that would become the best of friends and traveling companions began to grow.

But not before more groups of passengers boarded the boat, stared at the three of us, and decided that their Mekong River cruise would be better if they were as far away from the three of us as possible.

"Your loss," I would say, as groups of people chose to bypass us and continue to fill up the back of the boat, where all the other boring people were silently waiting for them.

But with every boring person that entered the boat, another person would decide they wanted to join the party at the front.

Before long our group consisted of Sarah, a solo traveler from New York, Ashley and Greg, a sickeningly beautiful couple from Australia, Jake, a young, hysterical solo traveler from Texas, and two Dutch girls from Amsterdam, who were extraordinarily hungover from the previous night, but didn't let that stop them from being the second customers at the bar, grabbing some beers, and joining the front of the boat crew.

As the boat began to fill, the seating options grew more limited. There were a few random seats left, and the boat was scheduled to leave in minutes. The late stragglers were now left without options and had to take whatever seats were available.

Luckily, for the final two passengers to board the boat, there was just enough room for them to squeeze next to our group, and without any choice, Murray and Alistar a pair of college roommates from Scotland and England respectively were the final members of our Slow Boat crew.

As the boat launched and we began floating down the Mekong River the passengers at the back of the boat began to wake up, take notice of the fun that the front of the boat was having, and quickly realized that they made a huge mistake.

One by one, people began making their way up to the front of the boat, introducing themselves, and sharing their disappointment that they were stuck in the back, missing out on all the fun of getting to meet people from all over the world and sharing the incredible journey with new friends.

We began to squeeze even closer together, making room for new members to join the group. People began sitting on the floor, surrounding us. People were even sitting on the ledge of the boat, straddling the rail, essentially risking their lives, just to join in on the front of the boat fun. Many of them would join us bearing gifts in the form of as many beers as they could carry that they just purchased from the cooler at the bar.

Before long, the front of the boat turned into an impromptu cocktail party. But instead of cocktail party attire, we were all dressed in the clothes that many of us had been wearing for days. And instead of cocktails, we were all drinking extra large, moderately chilled, BeerLao beers. And instead of friends gathering after work, we were strangers from all over the world, floating down a river in Laos.

Due to overcrowding at the front of the boat, the party inevitably began spreading throughout the rest of the boat. Each time one of us ventured to the back of the boat to grab more beers for the crew, a new passenger would say to us "You guys are having a blast up there, aren't you?" to which we would reply, "Come on up and join us."

This included Alberto, a loud, dynamic, hysterical Italian, who physically cringes each time I butcher his name with my American accent. And Antoine from France, who if was any more laid back he would be in a coma.

Hours passed and as people began shifting around and making sure they introduced themselves to each member of the group, we realized that we were already halfway through the first leg of the trip.

Suddenly, almost as if it were a referee blowing a whistle informing us that it was halftime, we got bombarded by a Canadian solo traveler so enthusiastic and outgoing that we all stopped our conversations and focused on him.

He was the life of the party, insisting that we all take a shot of his Laotian liquor that he had purchased before boarding. He was so pumped up to finally be a part of the front of the boat that he never even told anyone his name. He was simply referred to as "Canada."

Canada refused to sit still, instead choosing to spread his love throughout the boat, offering each and every person shots of his mysterious Laotian liquer.

Every so often someone would say "Where is Canada?," or "Who is Canada making take shots now?" or "Has anyone checked up on Canada lately to make sure that he is still alive and hasn't fallen off of the boat?"

As if on cue, Canada would reappear, making sure that anyone that wanted to take another shot, was well supplied.

"Don't worry, eh, there is plenty more where that came from, eh," Canada would assure us, each time the bottle grew empty.

Hours later, as I was making my way back from purchasing a new round of beers for my new friends, I walked past Canada talking to a shy, quiet couple, in the middle of the boat.

This is all I heard of the conversation as I walked by…

"I love you guys. I mean, neither one of you are THAT great individually, but together as a couple, you guys are amazing."

Upon hearing this, the couple looked at each other, looked at Canada, and slowly said "Thank you?" confused about whether they should take the statement as a compliment or an insult.

I shared the story with the front of the boat crew, and that was the official moment that Canada became a living legend on the slow boat cruise.

By the time the boat dropped us off for our overnight stay in Pakbeng, we were no longer strangers, but a buzzed group of friends from all over the world. After checking in to our respective guesthouses, we gathered as a group for dinner and karaoke before returning back to our guesthouses and getting some much needed rest.

We were all moving a bit slower the next morning as we made our way to the boat for the second day of our journey to Luang Prabang, Laos. None of us more so than Canada, who needless to say was the very last person to board the boat.

He waved off all of our cheers as he boarded the boat, and with his head down, he proceeded to the rear of the boat, laid on the floor, and stayed there for the entire eight hours of our travels, completely blocking the pathway to the back of the boat, where passengers would gather to get some air, have a smoke, or take in all the views of the Mekong River.

Sure, he caused a massive human traffic jam for a solid eight hours, but nobody was really bothered by this. Everyone would simply say "Oh, that's just Canada, what a fun guy," as they awkwardly stepped over his lifeless body.

The slow boat journey costs about 1/20th of a Royal Caribbean 3-day cruise, and may not have the amenities that a cruise ship offers, but the experience of floating down the Mekong River with strangers from all over the world far surpasses anything that Royal Caribbean could ever possibly offer.

21. Laos Luxury Budget Water...FALL Disaster

Perhaps the most fascinating thing about Laos is that the country itself can make you feel like you are on a luxury vacation, even when you are backpacking and staying at hostels. The sheer beauty of the place makes you want to explore each and every inch of it and discover hidden gems, as well as the places well known for being breathtaking.

Laos is not a country where a "luxury budget" is needed to get the most out of your experience. In fact, I would almost recommend against spending time in "luxury" when you are in Laos, for fear that you will miss out on the authenticity of the culture and the plethora of natural beauty the country has to offer.

With that being said… one thing you should certainly not skip out on when in Laos, particularly its capital, Luang Prabang, is having your own access to transportation. Going where you want, when you want, and not having to worry about how you are getting there, is crucial in a place that has so many off the beaten path, must-visit, experiences.

Should you opt for a luxury accommodation, however, you can get a 5-star hotel with a mountain view balcony for around $70 USD per night. And if you are really looking for some top notch luxury, for about $120 per night (sometimes even less), you will quite literally get A-list celebrity treatment if you stay at a resort such as Avani+, which is where I was residing for my time in Laotian luxury.

Avani+ offers all the amenities that any 5-star resort would offer, including spa treatments, fine dining options and a full length swimming pool. Additionally, it is centrally located to all the Luang Prabang hot spots, including the main market and the Mekong River.

But what made my luxury days in Laos most memorable was the fact that the resort offered excursions to some of Luang Prabang's most popular attractions. After boarding a river cruise which took me (I was flying solo for the moment) downstream to the village of Ban Muang Khai, a driver was waiting to take me the remaining few kilometers to our destination; the Kuang Si Waterfalls.

The Kuang Si Waterfalls is a three tiered waterfall that is so beautiful that you will feel like you have stumbled upon the set of "Blue Lagoon." The majority of the pools at the falls are open for the public to swim in with the exception of one of them considered to be sacred.

Staring at the glistening layers of turquoise blue water cascading onto each other in a hypnotic rhythm is guaranteed to be a sight and sound that you will remember for the rest of your life.

Moments after I entered the grounds of the Kuang Si Waterfalls, I met a young French couple that had already explored the falls and were relaxing in an area they deemed to be the best spot in the house; it offered easy access to enter into the pools and was surrounded by a view that will quite literally make you forget to breathe.

After listening to the advice of the couple and plopping down next to them, I began disrobing and prepping to take my relaxing dip into the crystal clear waters. As I was settling in, the couple kept telling me to be careful because the rocks were extremely slick and they were slipping and sliding all over the place, and even pointed to scratches on their knees and elbows as if they were trying to convince me that they were not exaggerating.

This is in line with all the other advice I had received from friends that had already visited the falls.

"Watch your step getting in and out," said one friend. "Pay attention to where you are walking, we fell," said another group of travel friends.

How the slippery can these rocks be, I kept repeating to myself. *Have these people never walked on wet rocks before? What the hell is wrong with these people?*

But, heeding the advice from all those that made the venture into the falls before me, I walked slower than a weakened geriatric patient into the falls until finally my feet were no longer reaching the alleged "rocks of doom," and let my body collapse gently into the refreshing waters. Never once did I feel even the slightest sign of a slip.

Amateurs. The whole lot of them. I said out loud, as I began frolicking through the waters.

Every time I floated past a fellow waterfall attendee, I would make the same small talk with them. First I would say something along the lines of "It's so beautiful, isn't it?"

To which they would respond with something like "It is the most amazing thing I have ever seen."

Then I would say "Did you find the rocks to be slippery? Because I didn't and everyone I spoke to told me that the rocks were going to be extremely slippery."

And each person replied, "Oh my gosh, that was so scary. I was sliding all over the place."

Huh, I would say out loud each time.

This same conversation kept repeating itself with each new person I met, until finally, after an hour or so, I decided it was time to get out of the water and rejoin my French friends that I met for about one minute but already decided when we inevitably exchanged phone numbers they would be in my contacts as "ViVi and Jacques France Laos Waterfalls."

I started making my way towards the place where I entered the falls, but noticed a big human traffic jam of people walking like Antarctic penguins, and decided I wanted nothing to do with that mayhem, so I swam to the nearest edge that looked like a suitable exit from the waters.

But here, instead of walking up rocks like you would exit an inground pool via the stairs, I had to use my arms to hoist my body out of the falls, much like the way you would exit an above ground pool without using the ladder.

As I placed my hands on the rocks, I realized that they did feel a bit slippery and slimy, but didn't really think much of it. When I hoisted my body up my right hand slipped out from under me, allowing my right elbow, followed by my head, to crash right down on the rocks.

I frantically looked around and played it off by laughing to myself and yelling "I'm fine," to whoever the hell was listening or cared.

I dipped below the water again. Half because I was mortified and was considering drowning myself, and half to wash off any blood that was probably dripping down my head.

I shook out my arms and attempted to exit again… only to have the exact same thing happen. After the second attempt though, my elbow was bleeding hard. It looked like a scene from Jaws, what with all the blood floating around.

I was about to give it one third and final attempt before admitting failure and getting out by way of the elderly penguins still inching along the normal exit, when a nice British man, I would imagine to be in his early sixties, walked by and extended his hand to help me out.

"Thanks so much, but I am all set. I got this," I said to the man in his sneakers, khaki shorts well below his knees and button down short sleeve "Hawaiian style" Laotian shirt.

But the man would not retract his hand.

Damn stubborn Brit, I thought to myself as I thanked him for his support in helping me out of the water.

I grabbed his wrist as he grabbed mine and he hoisted me out of the water with ease.

But as my feet landed on the rocks they immediately went out from under me and I fell right back into the water.

Still holding the 60 year-old British man's wrist for support, he too, plunged in right after me. Fully clothed with his big fat wallet filled with Laotian money and presumably pictures of his lovely grandchildren, he was now unexpectedly swimming in the Kuang Si Waterfalls.

As we both began swimming towards the proper exit that I should have taken originally, I am pretty sure I broke the world record for how many times a person has said "I am so sorry," in a two minute period.

All eyes were on the two of us, as we inched our way out of the falls. I hugged the man, told him I would give him money to replace his now ruined money, and even offered my dry clothes for him to change into, all of which he adamantly denied.

I could not get out of the grounds quick enough. All I wanted to do was run back to my belongings, grab everything and get the hell out of there, never to be seen by any of the witnesses ever again.

But I had to walk slow, because the last thing I needed was to fall again.

After what seemed like hours, though it was probably about a minute, I was back at my towel and my French friends that were horrified by my bleeding elbows and knees.

"We told you. And you did not listen to us," they said in their thickest French accents, just to be even more dramatic.

"I am going to head back to my resort now and not leave the comfort of the pool and lounges for at least two days," I joked. You guys can stop by later if you are in the area, as long as you never mention what you just saw ever again in your life.

They agreed they would come join me in luxury later.

I threw on my shirt, and sat down to dry my feet. I made sure there was not a drop of water on them. I was essentially scrubbing them dry to ensure I didn't fall again.

I then meticulously put on my socks. And after literally scrubbing the bottoms of my shoes with my towel, placed my sneakers on my feet.

I threw my blood soaked towel in my bag and stood up to say goodbye to my French friends. As I took my VERY first step to head back to my driver, I stepped on the most slippery rock in Asia and my legs came out from under me and I fell on my ass harder than I have ever fallen in my life.

After his fits of hysterics subsided, Jacques helped me up, brushed off my back, and after saying "Ryan from America, you must be very careful here. I told you. But you are a very funny guy," sent me on my way, one miniscule step at a time, back to my ride to begin my physical and mental recovery process in the safety of my luxury Laotian resort.

22. Cuba - Low Budget Rum'ing in the Rain

Until recently, the thought of an American vacationing in Cuba was unheard of. With extreme limitations in place prohibiting our ability to visit the island nation for decades, visiting Cuba has always been a goal of mine that seemed unattainable.

So when I walked out of the Jose Marti International Airport in Havana, Cuba an almost unearthly feeling came over me. The country is relatively frozen in time, and visiting Cuba is the closest one will likely ever get to time travel. With cars cruising by from the 1940's and 50's, many of which are in pristine condition, it is difficult to not feel like you are an extra in a James Dean movie.

After an initial night exploring Havana, I spent the remainder of my low budget days in the beautiful city of Trinidad, Cuba, which I reached by way of a 1954 Chevy. After the novelty of riding in such a classic car wore off, I quickly realized that it was going to be a long, uncomfortable five hours in a car with no air conditioning that doesn't pass speeds of 50 miles an hour, but I did my best to embrace my surroundings and make the most of the experience.

Naturally, my driver did not speak a single word of English, and I spoke about 20 words of Spanish, so it was a very quiet, awkward ride that seemed like it would never end. But eventually we ended up in Trinidad and my driver deposited me at a casa particular (guest house) owned by a woman named Alicia (who also spoke zero words of English.)

Alicia was in her mid sixties and even though we did not speak the same language, I understood enough Spanish to know that she was already overly protective of me and would take excellent care of me for the four days I would be staying at her house. She fed me, did her best to give me directions, and like my own mother and grandmother, told me not to drink too many cervezas when I ventured out into town. But after a ride like the one I just experienced, I could make no promises.

So with a full belly and utterly useless walking directions that I pretended I understood, but didn't, I left Alicia's house to explore the beauty of Trinidad.

The city of Trinidad, along with the neighboring Valle de los Ingenios (Valley of the Sugar Mills) is considered a UNESCO World Heritage Site. For years, sugar trade was the main industry in Trinidad, but today it is very much tobacco processing, which I took full advantage of by stuffing every square inch of room in my bag with cheap, authentic Cuban cigars.

Since it is a UNESCO World Heritage Site, the city is well preserved and the main city center is clean, organized, and welcoming with colonial cobblestone streets that you will undoubtedly twist both of your ankles on multiple times over the course of your stay if you are anything like me.

It is entirely possible to spend multiple days exploring the nooks and crannies of Trinidad and spend next to nothing to keep yourself entertained. One of the major highlights is the Casa de la Musica (House of Music). Many cities in Cuba have their own Casa de la Musica, but Trinidad's is a bit unique as it is spread over a long set of stairs leading up from the main plaza.

Picture the Spanish Steps in Rome, but with music, drinking, dancing and socializing rather than simply sitting on them and taking selfies. Nearly every visitor is enjoying a Cuba libre (rum and coke), daiquiri, or mojito while relaxing with a local Cuban cigar.

Live music blares from the streets and steps, and each night is celebrated with friends and family. It is a popular hangout during the day, but the real action takes place once the sun goes down.

So while exploring the city, I made a few cheap purchases to enhance my visit to Trinidad, including my Cuban cigars and two bottles of Havana Club rum, one for myself to enjoy on the rooftop during my stay at my casa particular, and the other as a gift to take back home for my brother. My plan was to check out the Casa de la Musica for a little while, see what all the fuss was about and then head back to Alicia's to get a good night of rest before my first full day of exploring the city.

I reached the Casa de la Musica right before sundown and as I sat on the steps and ordered a mojito from a waitress, I took out one of the Cuban cigars and lit it up.

But before I could even take my first puff, I felt a raindrop on my cheek. I looked behind me to see if anyone else was reacting to getting rained on, and saw people frantically running for cover, much like the wedding scene in the music video for "November Rain" by Guns N' Roses.

My instincts told me to run for cover, but I didn't want the waitress to come back with my mojito and not be able to find me; with my luck I would have been arrested for ditching out on a bill and thrown into a Cuban prison for the rest of my life (best case scenario.)

So I stood there, waiting in what has now become a downpour, like the American idiot I am. If you have ever been through a treacherous thunderstorm in Florida that comes out of nowhere and feels like the end of the world, picture that but about three times worse. That is what was happening around me as I was now the only person sitting on the Casa de la Musica steps that up until a few minutes ago were jam packed with people.

I waited for what seemed to be the longest three minutes of my life, and realized that there was no way my waitress would ever even consider that I would still be sitting on the steps waiting for a mojito in the middle of an impromptu tropical storm, so I slowly walked down the steps to head back to Alicia's, looking back every three or four steps to make sure the waitress and what I would imagine to be her Cuban mafia family, were not running behind me with a baseball bat.

Eventually I was able to round the corner and slip out of view from the crowd of people staring at me from under awnings, safely hidden from the rain. Instead of focusing on how many seconds it would take my parents to drop dead upon hearing the news that I would never be able to leave a Cuban jail cell for the rest of my life because I didn't pay for a mojito I ordered but never received, I could now focus my attention on making my way back to my casa particular.

But there was a problem… I had no clue how to get back to my casa particular.

WiFi is non-existent in much of Cuba. And the English language is not much more prevalent.

So I was left with my memory, and with the task of backtracking my steps back to Alicia's on my own. Spoiler alert… Due to my undiagnosed ADD, I am pretty much useless at remembering directions and backtracking steps.

The only tool I had to help was a picture of an AirBnB receipt that I had for Alicia's place, which gave not the exact address, but a vicinity in which her place was located.

A few blocks into my journey back I heard a man shout "Gringo! A donde vas?," which I somehow knew meant "Hey white man, where are you going?"

I responded by saying "Amigo, donde esta, Alicias?," as if there was only one Alicia in Cuba.

The man called me up to his porch and asked me the same question, this time leaving out the "gringo" part, which I was thankful for.

I took out my phone and showed him the picture of the area I believed Alicia lived. The man gave a bunch of "Ohhhhhhhh's" and "A-haaaaaa's" that I didn't need to break out Google Translate for. He had no idea where it was, but he was going to attempt to point me in what he believed to be the right direction.

I said "Muchas gracias" about 90 times and as a thank you, offered the man one of my bottles of rum that I purchased.

He said something along the lines of "Me sip, you sip," and so I opened a bottle, took a big swig of straight rum, and handed the bottle to the man who did the same.

He handed the bottle back to me, patted me on the back, and said "Adios, amigo" followed by something else that I did not understand but assumed meant "Good luck finding that place in this pouring rain, you dummy."

After another obnoxious string of "Muchas gracias'" I waved goodbye and ventured back out into the tropical storm.

During all the hoopla of the past 15 minutes I realized I must have dropped my soaking wet cigar that I didn't get to have, because it was nowhere to be found.

Great, I thought to myself, *add another reason to the list of Cuban imprisonment; littering in a World Heritage Site.*

But there was no time to worry about that again, I needed to get my ass back to Alicia's before the trip was cut 5 months short due to me catching pneumonia.

I walked for a while until I saw two boys in their late teens or early twenties, on a porch. Nearly the exact same thing happened with these kids… I showed them a picture of the vicinity, they pretended like they knew where it was, I offered them some rum, we all took swigs, and I left, having no better insight as to where I was supposed to be heading.

I walked in circles around the neighborhood I thought Alicia's house was in, but nothing seemed familiar.

Just as I was about to consider asking my porch friends for the nearest estacion de policia (police station) and turn myself in for all my crimes, in exchange for a warm, dry, cell block, I heard "Amigo! amigo!" It was one of the kids that was on the second porch I visited, riding a bicycle.

He approached me, asked to see the picture on my phone again, inspected the photo for a few seconds, handed me my phone back, and tapped his bike seat, instructing me to hop on and straddle him to what I was praying was Alicia's house.

This 20-year old Cuban and I were racing through the streets of Trinidad, completely soaking wet, and embracing each other on a bike that was way older than he was. If there was a picture of this, I am sure it could be used as some sort of cover art for the next softcore romance novel by Danielle Steel.

He eventually found Alicia's house, and it turns out HE KNEW HER, as she opened the door and embraced him, and slapped me on the top of the head with her dishrag.

"CERVEZAS!," she yelled at me, before inviting my rescuer in to dry off. He graciously refused the offer to come inside, but he did accept my offer to finish my bottle of rum with me.

After we polished off the bottle, I said "Screw it" and handed him my second bottle of Havana Club rum that I bought. I insisted he take it back to his friend and enjoy it together.

We hugged about eight times and I said "Muchas gracias, amigo! Buenas Noches!"

At that point in my journey I did not yet know how to say "Thank you for saving my life, my friend. I love you," in Spanish, but if I did, you can be sure I would have been yelling it off the rooftop porch as my new Cuban hero disappeared on his bicycle into the tropical storm, waving his very own bottle of Havana Club rum into the air.

23. Cuba - Moderate Budget Hemingway's Paparazzi

American novelist and short story writer, Ernest Hemingway first visited Havana, Cuba back in 1928 while on a layover during a trip to Spain. It only took him two days to become obsessed with the city. When he returned four years later, he decided he would on and off live there for nearly the rest of his life, which as it turns out was over thirty years.

One of the places that sparked his love affair with the city of Havana was the Ambos Mundos Hotel, which is still a highlight of Havana today. It was in room 511 of this hotel, years later, that Hemingway would write three novels while standing up, due to his bad knees on account of an old injury he attained in World War I.

Hemingway quickly became a legend in Havana, with locals affectionately dubbing him "papa" due to his grey beard and father-like persona. Eventually he became so intertwined with Cuba that he referred to himself as a "Cubano Sato," which basically translates to a "pure Cuban."

When Fidel Castro became the Prime Minister of Cuba in 1959, it didn't take long for Hemingway and his family to leave the country and return to live in the United States. There is much debate as to if Hemingway was forced to leave Cuba in 1960, or whether he was so displeased with the direction in which Cuba was headed and left on his own accord, but less than a year after he departed Cuba for the final time, Ernest Hemingway committed suicide at the age of 61.

Hemingway felt at home in Cuba, and it is where he wrote some of his most beloved work, including *For Whom the Bell Tolls* and *The Old Man and the Sea*.

So, needless to say, Ernest Hemingway's favorite hangouts are hot commodities to visit in Havana. Since I was traveling in Havana on a moderate budget, a stay at the Ambos Mundos was not in the cards. A visit to the hotel, including a rooftop lunch and afternoon cocktails, however, was very much in the cards.

As a writer, it is almost surreal to be on the same rooftop that Ernest Hemingway was on, and staring at the views that he stared into while writing some of the most beloved pieces of American literature ever written.

But since my time in Havana was limited, I needed to make the most of it, and obsessing over Ernest Hemingway for four days and not getting the full, authentic Havana experience would have been a crying shame.

So I ventured out to explore the wonders of Havana, including an 8km (5mi) walk down the entire stretch of the Malecon, the legendary seawall that stretches along the coast of Havana. Construction on the wall began in 1901 in order to protect Havana from the sea, but today, 120 years later, while it is obviously still being used as protection from the sea, it doubles as a popular gathering spot for locals to congregate each night to enjoy a few cervezas and chat about the days events. Additionally, it is also known to be a hotspot for both male and female Cuban prostitution, if you are into that sort of thing. And let's be honest, who isn't?

For a few USD you can grab some highly regarded Havana pizza and some Cuban Cristal beers, make your way to the

Malecon, and be thoroughly entertained each and every evening of your stay in Havana.

Another must visit attraction in Havana is the Hotel Nacional de Cuba, built in 1930. It has since become a national monument and a symbol of history, culture and Cuban identity. The Hotel Nacional de Cuba has such a refined elegance to it that many notable celebrities and political leaders have chosen to call it home during their time in Havana.

Marlon Brando, Frank Sinatra, Ava Gardner, Fred Astaire, Johnny Weismuller, Leonardo DiCaprio, and even Walt Disney are some of the names that have been guests at the hotel, along with British Prime Minister Winston Churchhill, Russian president Vladimir Putin, and former US president, Jimmy Carter to name a few.

The hotel sits on the grounds of where much of the spying took place during the Cuban Missile Crisis. The tunnels used to spy on the US, as well as the periscopes are still there today, and free to tour on the grounds of the hotel.

After a few days of completing the long list of Havana's must-visit attractions, I would be remiss, as a writer, to not take advantage of all the inspiration that Havana had to offer. So, in an attempt to channel my inner Hemingway, I decided to make my own personal Hemingway tour; making sure to visit all of his favorite writing spots, restaurants, and perhaps most importantly, bars. After all, he once famously said...

"Don't bother with churches, government buildings, or city squares. If you want to know about a culture, spend a night in its bars."

It is no secret that Ernest Hemingway liked to drink. In fact, Hemingway was known for getting up extremely early in the morning to start writing (while standing because of that war injury.) He would write feverishly for hours, but by the time 11am rolled around, he was completely parched. So after a hard morning's work under his belt, he would typically head to one of his favorite watering holes, most often, the now world renowned, El Floridita.

Hemingway's niece, Hilary, has stated that in the early 1930's Ernest walked into El Floridita for the first time to use the toilet. While he was there, he overheard people bragging about the daiquiris, so he asked for one. He finished it and told the bartender, "One more, but this time with less sugar and more rum."

And with that, the Papa Doble, "papa" because of the nickname Hemingway had taken on in Cuba, and "doble" because it contained *double* the amount of rum, was born.

Hemingway loved the cocktail so much that he was known to easily down up to a dozen in one sitting, and it's common knowledge in Havana that he once took down 17 daiquiris in one day. In his book *Islands in the Stream* his protagonist, who coincidentally also loved the art of drinking, says (about the daiquiri) …

"This frozen daiquiri, so well beaten as it is, looks like the sea where the wave falls away from the bow of the ship when she is doing thirty knots.... No taste of alcohol and felt, as you drank them, the way downhill glacier skiing feels running through powder snow and, after the sixth and eighth, felt like downhill glacier skiing feels when you are running uproped."

Needless to say, he was a big fan.

Now simply referred to as the Hemingway Daiquiri, people from all over the world come to El Floridita just to try the famous drink. In fact, when I walked through the doors at 11:30 a.m. on my third day in Havana, it was so crowded that not only was the bar standing room only, but the line circling the bar was three people deep.

I eventually was able to inch my way to the bar, and after a bit of hawkeye scrambling, even managed to grab a bar stool to order my much anticipated Hemingway Daiquiri. Through no fault of my own, my expectations were through the roof. After years of waiting to try the cocktail made famous by one of my literary heroes, the time had finally arrived.

I ordered my Hemingway Daiquiri from the bartender and less than a minute later, my daiquiri was in front of me. The bartenders at El Floridita could make these in their sleep.

Before I took my first sip I said to myself, *come on, Ryan, how good could this thing possibly be. Don't be too disappointed if it isn't the best thing you have ever tasted in your life. Afterall, it is Cuba and they are like a million and a half years behind the rest of the world.*

But after the first sip, I was hooked like Hemingway. It was, without a doubt, the best sip of anything I have ever taken in my life. I instantly grew an even deeper emotional bond with Hemingway, and felt bad about ever having judged him for drinking 17 of these in a day. After all, they aren't *that* big.

It wasn't until I had my daiquiri in my hands that I began to relax and take in my surroundings. El Floridita was the quintessential Havana gathering spot, which has become tarnished by tourists and bus loads of people coming in just to take a few pictures and clog up the place.

I felt almost sorry for adding to the problem of oversaturating the establishment with tourism, but consoled myself with the knowledge that at least I was buying daiquiris and giving the place actual business. Plus, I was only one man sitting in the corner of the bar, minding my own business and doing my best to stay as low maintenance as possible.

As I was scoping out the joint trying to force myself to take the smallest sips humanly possible so I didn't have to bother the bartender and immediately order another daiquiri, I couldn't help but notice the ridiculous amount of tourists taking pictures of me.

As a solo American world traveler, I wasn't too frazzled by the "paparazzi," as I have become quite accustomed to being stopped on the streets and asked for a photograph in places like Uganda, India, Sri Lanka, Laos, and most recently Cuba, simply for being white.

But something felt different about the amount of attention I was gathering here at El Floridita. Literally groups of people would walk through the doors, look around the place, see me, and whip out their cameras for their photo shoots. I knew I stuck out like a sore thumb in Havana, but I hadn't realized just how much until I was minding my own business trying to get Hemingway-too-drunk at El Floridita.

It became so awkward that I didn't know what to do, so I asked for the check, and decided to visit the remainder of Hemingway's favorite places, but promised the bartender (as if he gave a shit), and myself I would get back to El Floridita the next day right when the doors opened for business, and see what kind of damage I could do trying to beat Hemingway's daiquiri record.

As luck would have it, the next morning I received a message from a friend of mine, Kristen, saying that she had just arrived in Havana and knew I was there and wanted to meet up. In perhaps the most bizarre turn of events, Kristen is also from the small state of Rhode Island, but we had actually never spent a single day in the United States together. We had randomly met seven months prior in Lisbon, Portugal, and remained in contact since. You know what the famous philosopher, Mickey Mouse always says, "Though the mountains are wide, and the oceans divide, it's a small world after all."

So I asked Kristen to meet me at El Floridita promptly at 11:00 a.m. for opening time. I walked in, along with about 25 other people all more eager than the next to get a seat at the bar, and was lucky enough to manage to sit in my exact same seat as the day before.

I put my backpack down on the stool next to me in hopes that Kristen would arrive soon.

SPOILER ALERT: She didn't.

But guess who did arrive. The paparazzi. Again.

Once again groups of people would walk through the doors, take a good look around the place, and then focus their cameras right on the American man drinking Hemingway Daiquiris by himself at El Floridita. I began to panic a bit because I had no phone service and no way of reaching Kristen to tell her I was being stalked and would like to switch locations.

So I sat there, drinking my daiquiris, being photographed as if I was an A-list celebrity walking through LAX airport who just got caught having an affair with a much younger co-star while my wife, who is eight months pregnant, is volunteering in Haiti rebuilding homes and spending her free time reading to hospice patients.

Luckily Kristen arrived just as I was finishing my second daiquiri (I promise mom, these things really are tiny.)

We exchanged *holas* and shared a few hugs, and she gave a few lame excuses about why she was late which I don't remember. Then once the pleasantries were out of the way, I whispered to her.

I will order you one daiquiri. Drink it as fast as you can. Then we are getting the fuck out of here.

I sounded like I was a fugitive on the loose, and she looked at me as if she was thinking just the same.

"What? Why? I thought you wanted to try and break Hemingway's record. I thought you loved these daiquiris? Why do you want to leave?" Kristen asked, puzzled.

I pointed to the wall of people standing in front of the bar and said "Everyone is taking pictures of me. It is insane, and getting really annoying."

Kristen looked at the paparazzi, then slowly looked at me. "What. The. Hell? Why are they taking hundreds of pictures of you?" she said without moving her lips.

I simply shrugged my shoulders and said..

"See. Told you," through gritted teeth.

Because while I was unbelievably annoyed at what was taking place, I still, admittedly, wanted to look good in these pictures. After all, I am basically representing an entire country.

So my entire time during the two days I was at El Floridita I was basically pretending to be a model. When I was alone and had nothing left to pretend to fiddle with, I would stare off pensively into the restaurant, always doing my best to let the cameras get what I know are my better angles.

When I was with Kristen, I would talk, and listen, and laugh, as if I was a silent film star… always mindful of the camera, but never letting my awareness be known.

We got our daiquiris (Kristen her first, mine the third) and raised our glasses together to cheers not only to Hemingway, Havana, and Cuba, but also our long awaited reunion.

As she took her first sip of the world famous drink, we were still looking each other in the eyes, as it is the polite thing to do while in the midst of a "cheers" with someone.

Her eyes must have wandered behind my shoulder, because no sooner had she taken her first sip that I felt an ice cold mist spray my face.

It was her daiquiri.

Does she not like it? I said to myself.

Impossible. I determined.

"What the hell is wrong with you?" I finally said.

She didn't say any words, simply pointed behind my shoulder.

There, standing about two feet behind me, was a gigantic, life-sized bronze statue of Ernest Hemingway himself. Standing up at the end of the bar, on account of that old war injury that prevented him from being able to sit on a bar stool.

As it turns out, the people of Havana were not as obsessed with me as I had previously thought. In fact, I probably have quite a low approval rating from all the tourists that were in Havana those two days, as I am sure I ruined every one of their Ernest Hemingway at El Floridita pictures they have been waiting their whole life to snap.

On the plus side, however, this meant that we could stay at El Floridita and we did not have to leave due to me thinking I was being harrassed. I can not be sure if I broke Hemingway's record that day at El Floridita, but based on the way I felt the following morning, I must have come pretty damn close.

24. Cuba - Luxury Budget Luxury Ride to Nowhere

After eight days of getting the full Cuban experience by staying at casa particulars, eating street food, sightseeing important Cuban landmarks, and mingling with the locals, it was finally time to pamper myself, Cuban style.

Because Americans have had such a difficult time traveling to the country of Cuba for decades, the town of Varadero, Cuba is relatively unknown to the vast majority of us. But mention Varadero to Canadians and they will stop what they are doing, throw their hockey skates in the closet, herd their moose into the nearest barn, and start packing up their suitcases before they can say "Could you pass the poutine and maple syrup, eh?" in the most polite way possible, of course.

Varadero, Cuba is a stunningly beautiful beach resort destination located about two hours east of Havana, Cuba (more on that fun fact later.) If you are an American, do yourself a favor and Google Varadero, Cuba before you continue reading.

Also referred to as Playa Azul or Blue Beach, Varadero is one of the largest resort areas in the entire Caribbean, and it is ranked in many professional travel lists as one of the best beaches in the world.

I would be found negligent if I did not explore as many different facets of Cuban experiences as possible, so I booked a stay at an all inclusive resort right on the beach in Varadero, Cuba. I ordered another taxi collectivo (basically an uber that picks up multiple people and takes them on a relatively long road trip) and left Havana for Varadero.

Once again my driver spoke very limited English, but this time, he was a sweet old man, and wouldn't let our lack of sharing the same native language stop him from giving me the best taxi colectivo ride of my life.

It took him about an hour to convey to me that there was a popular Pina Colada stand on the way and ask me if I wanted to stop at it. After my night of imitating Ernest Hemingway, the very last thing I wanted to do was drink Pina Coladas, but alas, I conceded and we pulled over for some frozen fun. He was nearly jumping out of his seat with joy once I gave him permission to stop.

The layover consisted of the nice old Cuban man staring at me for a half hour while the same thing happened repeatedly. I would take a sip, say "Es bueno. Delicioso," and he would smile and yell back to the person, presumably his friend that made it and yell something in Spanish. Then I would give a "thumbs up" to the man that made it and yell "ES BUENO! DELICIOSO!" and while flashing a big smile and clutching his chest for some unknown reason, would yell something back to me in Spanish that I didn't understand.

After the pit stop it was pedal to the medal to get my ass to my all-inclusive resort by 3:00 p.m.. That is the time you could check in, and at which time could begin your "all-inclusiveness."

When I arrived at Be Live! all inclusive, I deposited my belongings in my room, grabbed a towel and my journal, and took off for the beach. Bypassing about seven open bars I was proud of my determination to get some work done while relaxing on the beach rather than drink the day away at the pool.

I am such an adult sometimes.

I rotated between journal writing on my lounge chair and swimming in the crystal clear turquoise blue waters for hours before deciding to shower, grab some dinner at one of the many all-you-can-eat restaurants, and retire to my room to have an early night and catch up on my writing.

On my way back to the room I decided to reward myself for all my hard work (i.e. laying on a beach and writing a few sentences, and putting on sunscreen after I got out of the ocean) and approached the bar to grab a free frozen drink to take to my room with me.

The Cuban sun is HOT. And a few minutes in it without protection will likely give you the sunburn of your life. This is something I had been warned about by the people of Cuba for the past week and a half, and I did not want to take any chances, so I was sure to lather up when exposed to the Cuban sun.

But you know who didn't heed this advice? The kid standing in line in front of me at the pool bar, Alex, from Canada.

Alex was so burned that I actually first thought that he was wearing a red long sleeved shirt. It wasn't until he turned around and I saw the pale white spaces in the indentations of his abs that I could tell just how badly he was burned.

I turned to the kid next to me and made fun of burned Canadian Alex, only to find out that he was his best friend, who assured me he had been making fun of Alex for days on end already as well.

Nothing bonds two strangers more quickly than making fun of somebody else, so I immediately became best friends with Mitch, the Canadian that did learn how to apply sunscreen to his body (although not properly, because he has the most bizarre pattern of sunburn I have ever seen beaming off his chest like a tattoo.) But it paled in comparison to Alex's so all my bullying efforts were focused on poor Alex.

I joined their crew at the poolside and as we continued to be in awe of Alex's skin, a new set of Canadian friends joined us, Elliot and Brendan and their families, as well as Alex and Mitch's friends Becca and Ethan. Rounding out the crew was eighteen year old Riley, who was vacationing with his mom (they, too, were Canadian.)

I quickly found out that I was the only American around (with the exception of a solo female traveler that everyone at the resort had affectionately already dubbed "the drunk old American lady" the night before I arrived.)

For two days I became part of the Canadian crew; eating all my meals with the Canadian twenty-somethings and their adult parents, and staying awake until the sun came up just chatting about travel, and life. But mostly about reality tv as they were massive *Big Brother* and *Survivor* fans. My people.

But because I had planned on visiting another part of Cuba for a few days before I flew to Mexico, I only booked two nights at the resort and would not be able to join my friends for the last two days of Varadero luxury.

I am not one who likes to miss out on any fun being had, so I booked a hotel next door (for one final night) at an even nicer all-inclusive resort, seeing as our hotel was booked. I checked in to the resort the following day, and immediately went back to spend the entire day with my Canadian friends.

I paid $200 for a piece of toast in the morning and a bed that I slept in for about two hours, then had to figure out how the hell I was going to get back to Havana for my flight to Cancun the next day.

I asked the concierge to book me a car to get to the airport and was told that it would be $150 because it was being booked so last minute and all they had was a very high end luxury classic car. *I'm an Idiot*, I said out loud, more to myself than to the concierge.

So I said my goodbyes to my Canadian family and got back to my resort just in time for my luxury ride to arrive. This time my driver spoke about 50 words of English, which is basically fluent as far as Cubans speaking English goes.

I told the man I needed to get to the airport for a 4:00 p.m. flight. It was noon, and the concierge assured me this would give me plenty of time to get to the airport and catch my flight.

The man smiled politely and said "We are off to the airport!"

"Si. Vamonos," I said, proud of my memory recall and using an appropriate Spanish word for a response.

About 20 minutes into the ride, the man pulled into the airport, ready to deposit me, and go about his day. I would imagine he was thrilled at the fact that he just made so much money for such a short trip.

"Is this the Havana airport?" I asked, confused about why this ride was much shorter than the ride to get to Varadero from Havana.

"This is Varadero airport," said the driver. "Havana is very far."

Shit, I said in my head, and then out loud.

"I need to go to Havana airport, amigo. My flight is at four."

"I can get you there by four, but we must go now," he said before adding "plus $100 more."

So I had no choice but to give the man another $100, this time instead of saying "Muchas gracias," three times, I said "Vamonos. Rapido. Mucho rápido," about ten.

An hour into the second leg of our adventure the man decided he wanted to buy me a Pina Colada.

What the hell is it about these Pina Coladas that these Cuban drivers are so obsessed with, I thought, but after he assured me we will still have time, he stopped at the exact same Pina Colada stand the other guy brought me to, and the exact same thing happened all over again.

I had to pretend it was the best thing I ever tasted, and then yell "Delicioso" to anyone that was staring at me. This time, however, I drank it as fast as I could, so I didn't miss my flight.

It was now approaching 2:30 p.m. and the driver still seemed confident I would make my flight, but my Google Maps that I had downloaded to my phone was suggesting otherwise.

As we got closer and closer to the airport, the clock got closer and closer to 4:00 p.m..

There was no way I was making this flight at this point, but I did not have it in my heart to tell the man, as we drove up to the airport exactly at 4:00 p.m., that my *flight* was at four, I didn't need to *arrive* at four.

So I pretended like everything was fine, went inside to confirm my flight had already left, and sat in the airport with no flight, nowhere to stay, and no way of getting WiFi to deal with any of these problems.

Just as I was considering voluntarily getting arrested in Cuba for the second time in two weeks, a Canadian family approached me.

"Eh… aren't you the America that was staying at our resort and hanging out with that really burned kid?" they said.

"Yup. That's me. Have you ever seen anyone more burned in your entire life? What the hell is wrong with him?" I said, unable to refrain from making fun of Alex one final time.

I explained my horrific situation to them, and they kindly let me use their WiFi to make arrangements for me to get picked up and taken to a casa particular by the airport.

I dramatically thanked them and invited them to America for Thanksgiving, which they politely declined and went out to meet my driver.

He took me to a casa particular, where I booked my new flight for the next day, and emailed my hotel in Cancun to tell them I would not be able to make it, as if they gave a shit, seeing as I already prepaid.

This was my biggest travel blunder to date, and to this day is still the most costly mistake I have ever made traveling.

Because of my fear of missing out on Canadian all inclusive hotel fun in Cuba, I spent the following…

- Extra night at an all inclusive resort. $200
- Ride to Varadero airport that I didn't need to go to. $150
- Ride from Varadero airport to Havana airport $100
- Extra night stay at Havana casa particular (including transportation and dinner.) $80
- Second flight from Havana to Cancun $120
- Loss of hotel for the night in Cancun. $175

I may have lost over $800 and a tremendous amount of respectability because I was making fun of a 21-year old's crab colored skin, but hey, at least I was now the proud owner of about 300 pictures of the inside of classic Cuban cars, a very good friend that sells Pina Coladas on the side of the road from Havana to Varadero, Cuba, and perhaps, most importantly, a perfectly bronzed tan.

25. Mexico - Low Budget World Wonder Tour Guide

Each year millions of tourists visit Chichen Itza in Mexico's Yucatan peninsula. It is believed that the large pre-Columbian city founded by the Maya people thrived from around the year 600 AD until approximately 1000 AD, and today is one of, if not the, most visited attractions in all of Mexico.

I arrived in Valladolid, Mexico by way of Cancun. And after the outrageously expensive fiasco that happened a few days before in Cuba, it was crucial for me to be even more frugal with my money (pesos) than normal low budget days.

Luckily for me, there were many free or low budget activities to do around Valladolid, the best of which was visiting one of their many beautiful cenotes. A cenote is a natural sinkhole that forms from the collapse of limestone bedrock which exposes groundwater underneath.

Some of the most beautiful cenotes in the world are known to be found in the Yucatan, and with an entry fee of just a few dollars, you can spend all day relaxing in its waters and drinking in the surrounding beauty.

So each day I would pack my day bag, including waters, snacks, my journal, and a few travel books and waste the days away in cenote happiness.

But, it is a crime to visit the Yucatan and not visit Chichen Itza; one of the Seven Wonders of the New World. So on my final day in Valladolid I splurged for the three dollar, 45-minute bus ride to Chichen Itza.

I made a promise to myself on this journey that I would try my best to stick to the allotted budget that I was assigned at each destination, and while the $13 admission fee to Chichen Itza didn't necessarily fall into the category of "cheap or free" it was certainly an acceptable purchase to have the experience of visiting my fourth World Wonder.

When I arrived at Chichen Itza the gates were not yet open, but the crowd of people had already formed, and the line only got longer with each passing minute. While standing in line, dozens of "official tour guides" walked by, asking each person if they wanted a "private tour," which, in addition to providing valuable information about the site, would allow them to bypass the line and gain immediate access inside.

Due to my budget restraints, I declined each offer and forced myself to wait in the slowest line on the planet, even as the mercury rose well past 100 degrees and no protection from the sun was available.

After an hour or so, I was finally at the ticket booth, at which time I paid my $13 USD and was asked about five more times if I would like to be part of a tour. Again, I politely declined.

I got my ticket, an utterly useless pamphlet describing the layout of the site, and I was off, ready to explore the World Wonder all on my own.

I quickly went up to the most well known of the attractions at Chichen Itza, El Castillo, and was able to grab about 20 selfies with nobody else in sight as they were too busy huddling around each other listening to their tour guides give a very well detailed account of anything that has ever happened there in the past 1500 years.

After my photoshoot with El Castillo I wandered around on my own, stopping at each attraction, staring at it for a few minutes, and then realizing I had no clue what I was looking at. I would then sashay on to the next attraction and repeat the process.

Eventually I decided that I should try to listen in to what all of the other tour guides were saying to their groups, as the people in these groups all seemed to be quite interested, even letting out occasional gasps of horror and/or excitement.

So I found a large group that had a bunch of white people in it as I figured that would be the group where I would stand out the least.

I casually kept my distance from then, but stayed close enough to them so I could get some fun facts.

Nothing makes you feel like a poor, pathetic loser more than trying to be a member of a tour group that people paid good money to be a part of, and knowing full well that each member of the groups knows that you didn't pay.

Each time I started receiving death stares from the paying members of the tour I would slowly wander off from the group and find a new one at the next attraction.

This process repeated a few times until I felt so awkward that I decided it was no longer worth the embarrassment.

So I tried looking up some information from the internet about what I was looking at, but the WiFi was so bad, and it was so hot, that it seemed like way too much work.

Then I got a brilliant idea. My friend Dan, who I assumed was at work not doing anything and was bored out of his mind, had been to Chichen Itza before. I can Facetime him, and he can give me a *very* brief summary of what I was looking at, and if he starts rambling on and on with details that I don't give a shit about, I can just start walking away and find something else that piqued my interest a bit more.

Or just hang up on him.

So I Facetimed him, and the plan worked like a charm. I would show him what attraction I was looking at, he would do a little research to confirm some facts, and would wrap it all up in about a 20-second summary. Knowing me so well, he would only include the facts that he knew I would deem to be entertaining (such as where people were sacrificed because others wanted it to rain so bad, or arenas where people would play a game like soccer, but the loser was decapitated,) you know, the fun stuff.

I ended up completing Chichen Itza in record breaking time, checking another World Wonder off my list, saving a bunch of money, and catching up with one of my best friends, all while preventing my undiagnosed ADD from ever even kicking in.

While on my way out I saw the first group I tried to join, all of them looking absolutely miserable and ready to drop dead of heat stroke and/or boredom, whichever would come first. I made sure they saw me wave to them as I was walking out the exit with an obnoxious, accomplished smile across my face.

26. Mexico
Moderate Budget
Sticking Out Like a Sore Yogi

"One of these things is not like the others
One of these things just doesn't belong
Can you tell which thing is not like the others
By the time I finish my song?"

Unless you lived a poor, sheltered life with no television and no access to the most iconic children's television show of all time, *Sesame Street*, you are probably familiar with their segment "One of these things is not like the others," which would typically give children four objects, three of which were exactly the same, and one of which was radically different.

The children then had to guess the thing that stood out, and Big Bird or one of his friends would congratulate them and explain to the stupid kids at home that didn't get the right answer, why, exactly, the fourth option stood out from the rest (i.e. maybe one of the bowls was significantly larger than the other three, or three of the objects were coconuts and one was Bert's rubber ducky.)

I have never seen an episode where a child guessed wrong, and how that would have played out for the show, but if anyone can find a link to an episode where a child could literally not figure out that three of the objects in front of him were rocks and one was a feather, kindly email me the link and I will send you a free copy of my next book.

Anyway, my moderate budget Mexican adventure took me to the town of Tulum, Mexico on the beautiful Caribbean coastline of the Yucatan Peninsula. Tulum is currently one of the hottest travel destinations, and many travelers are choosing to bypass other places, such as Cancun and Playa del Carmen in favor of Tulum.

Tulum is known for its pristine beaches (although in recent years seaweed concerns have been a hot button topic in the town,) breathtaking cenotes, iconic Mayan ruins, and world class nightlife.

Surviving on a moderate budget in Tulum was a non-issue since there are hundreds of moderately priced accommodation options, delicious food is relatively cheap, and there are many options for moderately priced activities.

Instead of staying on the beaches of Tulum, as I just spent four nights on the beautiful beaches of Varadero, Cuba just over a week ago, and would be spending my luxury time in Mexico on a beach as well, I decided to be a bit out-of-the-box and stay at Holistika, a holistic center, hotel, and community set in the middle of the Mayan jungle.

Holistika put a spin on the legendary Boston sport's bar, Cheers motto, by claiming it is a place where "Everybody knows your name, people know we are all the same, and they are always glad you came."

Well, I quickly found out that the first and third parts of that motto were legit; as everyone seemed to know my name in this holistic community, and they all seemed very happy that I came to stay there, but there was no denying that we were all definitely NOT the same.

Holistika is quite possibly the most peaceful, laid back, calming place I have ever been. Holistika "Sets the vibe to heal, balance, and reconnect with your deepest self and nature." They claim to be a "New way of dealing with everyday life and circumstances by purging, decodifying, and purifying the body through the flow of therapeutic healing arts."

Admittedly so, everything they "claim" is spot on and completely accurate. I very much plan on returning to Holistika for a vacation when I am not trying to squeeze in as much sightseeing, exploring, and writing as possible and fully enjoy the Holistika experience.

But with limited time to explore Tulum, my mind was constantly thinking of all the things I had to see and do, so there wasn't much time for reconnecting and finding my deepest self in the middle of the jungle. Also, do I even really want to "find myself?" knowing me, I am pretty sure I don't.

Plus, have I mentioned my complete inability to sit still?

Upon entering Holistika I was approached by three nauseatingly friendly hippies that were all wearing what I only know to refer to as MC Hammer pants. They all had dreadlocks, the two men shirtless, and the women had on a tank top that I believe was designed for a five year old. Do I even need to mention that none of them were wearing shoes?

They led me into the office and grabbed my bags, handed me some lemongrass water, whatever the fuck that is, and began asking me questions about my life. I told them I was a teacher back in the United States and was currently on a year-long project in which I was traveling around the world and writing about my experiences.

You would have thought I told them I had just invented the cure for cancer while simultaneously manning an exploration on

Mars by the way they reacted, as they all bowed to me and said, harmoniously, "sensei."

My nephew, Andrew, has been taking karate lessons since he was a small child, so I am familiar with the term sensei, and quickly assured them I am not a sensei and had only taken one yoga class in my life. And as far as my martial arts skills are concerned, I am quite literally a zero out of ten.

Then one of the guys said to me, "No, my friend, a sensei is a teacher; a master. You are an actual teacher, as well as a master writer and traveler. You are a sensei."

"Well… spoiler alert: I am not. Trust me," I said, trying to catch a glimpse of a hotel lobby bar or something. I could tell, I was going to need a drink if this silliness kept up.

The three wise yogis, as I liked to call them, then said they were off to their "Vinyasa Freedom" class with Debhany, and all said "Namaste, Sensei Ryan, thank you for coming," and disappeared into the jungle.

"Do they even work here?" I said to the woman checking me in.
"No," the woman said to me, shrugging her shoulders.

"Please do not put Sensei Ryan on any name tags that we presumably need to wear around here," I said to the woman.

"Trust me. I won't," she said, which made me laugh louder than anyone should, or probably has, ever laughed at a holistic yoga retreat center.

For two full days I never left Holistika. I stayed in the BeeHive, which is a 12-bedroom luxury dorm room in the shape of, you guessed it, a beehive.

I would eat breakfast, you guessed it again, avocado toast, and drink some sort of delicious detoxifying tea, while I wrote. Not that it is possible to get any work done there because all damn day you are forced to say "Namaste" to beautiful half naked people that are obsessed with saying "Namaste" to every person they can find.

Which leads me to my next point, I am not sure if holistic center hotels in the jungle make people sexy or if only sexy people stay at holistic center hotels in the jungle, but holy hell were these people all beautiful. There may be something to this lemongrass water, after all.

"Are you coming to Ashtanga Mysore with Yosef at 7:00 a.m., Sensei Ryan?" male hippy number one, Jonah, asked me.

"No, I have so much work to catch up on, I think I am going to wait for the 10:30 a.m. Bodhi Flow class with Tizia," I lied.

"Ok, then namaste," he said.

"Namaste," I replied, now panicking that Jonah was also going to go to the Bodhi Flow class with Tizia at 10:30 a.m. and not see me there.

Sure I could probably handle my own in one of these classes if they were geared towards beginners, which some are, but there was no way I was going to attend any single one of these classes in front of all these people that referred to me as Sensei Ryan.

So after breakfast I would grab my book and head to one of the pools at the center. I would spend the day floating in a pool in the middle of the jungle, mostly by myself because everyone else was either at a "Connecting Roots" seminar with Keith (why does he have such a normal name, I would ask myself every time I saw his name on a schedule,) or at MindSoul Expression with Jelena, or maybe even at the Kundalini Yoga and Gong Bath with Akal.

But I didn't care, because I was detoxifying my mind and body in my own way; by floating in a pool in the middle of the jungle and not partying my face off in Tulum.

Every hour, it seemed more and more, I was trying to avoid someone new because I had lied to them and told them I would see them in a class, or seminar, or bath or something, and I was always a no-show.

By day three I couldn't take being called Sensei Ryan anymore; I felt like a fraud. So I ordered an Uber and went to the beach area to check out what all the non-hippy tourists do in Tulum.

I explored the beaches, enjoyed happy hour(s) at the bars, met with locals and tourists alike, that gave me pointers on where to eat, what to drink, and what attractions were not to be missed.

Ahhhh, my people, I thought to myself, *how I have missed you.*

While at a beach bar, news broke that Luke Perry, the beloved *Beverly Hills 90210* actor that I admired so much as a child, passed away. I asked the solo traveler next to me if he knew who Luke Perry was.

"Dude, who doesn't know Luke Perry?" was his response.

Hallelujah, I thought to myself. *Finally, someone that gets me.*

So we chatted it up for an hour or so before I told him I was off to visit the Mayan ruins on the beach, which everyone has told me is a must-visit. He said he was about to go there too, so the bromance continued as we made our way to the ruins.

I asked him where he was staying, and he told me he has this "Really cool place near where we were." It was an eco-friendly hostel where "They made little hotel rooms out of large concrete tubes."

"Whoa that sounds neat," I said, jealous that he had his own concrete tube to stay in rather than feel guilty about not wanting to go to a Pranacore class at 7:00 a.m. with Dhyana.

Then he said… "I really wanted to stay at this place called Holistika, but they are all booked for the next two nights."

"No Shit! That is where I am staying and I would love to trade my stay in the jungle paradise for a concrete tube… let's switch," I said.

It took me about five more times of repeating what I had just said before he actually believed me. But once he finally realized I was serious, he was jumping with joy.

So after the ruins we took an uber to his concrete tube to get his belongings, and then another Uber to my place to get my things, and literally switched lives for two days.

We met for a drink on our final day in Tulum and he paid for my bill, saying that he could not believe that I made the switch and it was the best place he had ever stayed.

I thanked him for letting me stay in the concrete tubes, which just so happened to be located next to an amazing bar where I "found my inner self" by relaxing and listening to live music. We embraced, promising to keep in touch, which we never did.

As we were leaving, though, he told me that upon checkout the people at Holistika said "Did you enjoy your stay with us, Sensei Ryan?"

"You never told me you were a sensei," said Chad, the New Zealander that switched lives with me for two days.

"Oh yeah," I said, "I'll tell you all about how I became sensei the next time we see each other. It's a crazy story. YEARS of hard work and dedication," I yelled as I waved goodbye and got in my taxi to head to my luxury stay in Playa del Carmen.

27. Mexico - Luxury Budget
No Such Thing as a Free Meal

The Louvre, in Paris, France employs over 2,000 staff members, approximately 1,200 of which are security. There is even a team of 48 firefighters on call 24-hours a day, 7-days a week to protect Mona Lisa and her 37,999 friends.

Fort Knox, home to about half of the US gold reserve, is known to be the most heavily secured place on the planet. It is rumored that the grounds at Fort Knox are littered with landmines and electric fences. Additionally, machine guns supposedly go off when lasers are triggered, and the entire area is guarded by a radar.

And in case all that doesn't work, there are about 40,000 soldiers that call Fort Knox home and would be happy to help stop an unwelcome guest.

However, all of this security pales in comparison to Jose, the sole 80-year-old security guard at The Grand Riviera Princess All Suites Resort & Spa in Playa Del Carmen, Mexico.

When my taxi driver pulled into the resort to drop me off for my stay in Mexican luxury, security guard Jose was not having it. He asked me for my name, my passport, my reservation number, and even the last four digits of the credit card I used to purchase the room. Keep in mind this was all in Spanish, and by now you are aware of my limitations when it comes to the Spanish language. It was basically just a lot of pointing and shoulder shrugging.

Jose was not happy when I told him I had no idea what credit card I used, I didn't have any WiFi to look up my confirmation number, and my passport was at the bottom of my bag, but I knew my passport number and would kindly give it to him. Reminder: I was speaking in English, which might as well have been in Na"vi, the made up language used in Avatar, as far as Jose was concerned.

So he made me get out of my taxi; telling the taxi driver to "Espera ahi" which translates in English to "Wait right there."

Now that my taxi driver hated me too, the two of us had to sit there and wait for Jose to get back from his security booth and ask me a million more questions such as "Where are you coming from?" "How long are you staying?" and "Who is staying with you?"

After answering all the questions to the best of my ability, he let me into my resort without so much as an "Enjoy your stay" or however the hell you say "Enjoy your stay," in Spanish. I am not sure if Jose was like this while welcoming all of the resort's guests, but for some reason, he really did not want me to feel welcomed.

Luckily for me, the lovely front desk employee that was working at the time had a much more favorable opinion of me, and was wildly impressed when I told her about my travels and the project I was working on.

She upgraded my room to a deluxe poolside room that had stairs coming directly from my bedroom and down into the main pool, complete with a swim-up pool bar and all. Things were looking up for this guy.

I dropped off my bags in the room, opened the fully stocked, full-size refrigerator, ripped off my shirt and walked into the pool. Just twenty minutes prior I was being interrogated by the world's best security guard, and now I was living like a king at an all-inclusive resort.

For some bizarre reason, in my adult life, everytime I enter a swimming pool for extended stretches of time, I start to break out in hives. The hives typically go away about an hour after I get out, so it is not that debilitating of a disease to have. It is also like a built-in alarm clock telling me to get out and do something productive rather than swim around and try to become best friends with anyone that just so happens to be swimming in the same water.

Fun fact: when looking back at my year around the world, I would say a solid 60% of the friends I made were while swimming in some sort of water, but that is besides the point.

The Grand Riviera Princess Resort (yes, I am a grown man that stayed at a resort called 'The Princess' all by myself,) is enormous and every direction you look you will see pools with swim-up pool bars, food stands offering snacks and light meals of every variety, live activities and signs pointing to their own private beach.

Now that my brother, Cory, knows that I stayed at a place called The Princess, here is a good time to tell you that I went to the nearest pool bar and ordered a large captain and coke with an extra shot of whiskey on the side[3], just so he continues reading the book and doesn't completely judge me for the rest of my life.

I grabbed my drink and decided to go for a tour of the resort, trying to map out all of the places I would need to visit to make an informed decision about whether or not it would earn my recommendation.

After getting completely lost a handful of times, I stumbled upon an extraordinarily neat little restaurant, set way back on the beach, and secluded from the rest of the resort. Not only did the

---

[3] It was a strawberry daiquiri, but I don't think my brother knows how footnotes work.

restaurant look cozy and welcoming, but the restaurant's radio was blasting "Champagne Supernova" by Oasis from their loudspeakers. There was no way I was not going into this place.

So I walked up to the hostess and asked her if I could check out the place and decide if that is where I wanted to eat dinner. She happily agreed and let me stroll on through.

I took about three steps in, saw how beautiful the place was, and turned around, deciding that this was indeed, the place I would come back to for my all-inclusive dinner.

I thanked the woman, told her I would be back after I showered and changed for the night, and got lost about seven more times before I finally, by complete happenstance, stumbled upon my room, 83501A, perhaps the most convoluted, least user-friendly room number of all time.

I hastily showered and got all dressed up for my big night out at the Mexican luxury resort. The restaurant seemed nearly empty, and I was assuming now that the sun was about to start setting, people would start piling in to the coolest place on the property. Plus I had to allow some extra time for me to get lost a few more times.

By the time I finally got back to "The Chill Zone," the name of the fancy restaurant, I walked up to the same hostess, who confusingly asked me "You are alone?"

"Yup," I confidently told her, but followed it up by saying I was a writer, so I didn't look like a complete loser.

She was unimpressed, and likely still thought I was a complete loser, but I couldn't have cared any less at that point.

She walked me to my table and the six other couples, each dining with their significant other also stared at me as if I was a gigantic loser, so I whipped out my journal and started scribbling some nonsense so they knew I was a writer.

They too, were unimpressed.

As I was scribbling notes, the worst waiter on the planet came over and "greeted me" by saying…

"You know you have to pay for this. This is not part of the all-inclusive package."

Taken aback, I said "Umm. yeah, no kidding. Of course I know that."

I didn't know that.

So he returned a few minutes later with a menu, threw it on the table and said "And we only take cash," and walked away.

I was so stunned at how rude the man was, and what I possibly could have done to offend him, but I despise confrontation, so I said, "That is no problem, I have plenty of cash."

I lied again, but decided that was a problem for later.

I looked at the menu and had a mini stroke when I saw the astronomically high prices on the menu. But there was no way my pride was going to let me get up and not eat this meal.

I began feverishly taking notes, hoping that the waiter would see me and think I was important enough for him to start being nice to me.

It didn't work.

He came back over to me and said "Drink?"

So I asked him for a wine list. If this guy was going to think I was too poor to afford this dinner, I was going to prove him as wrong as I possibly could.

When I asked for the wine list, he said "We only do bottles, no glasses here."

"Yeah, I figured that," I said, as I lied to him for a third time.

When he returned with a wine list, he immediately said "What bottle of wine do you want," probably taking everything in his power to not call me "Dude" after everything he said to me.

I immediately eliminated the cheapest priced bottle on the menu, because I am sure that is what he would have predicted I would have ordered. So I went with about the fifth cheapest bottle on the menu, which was about $70; a small price to pay to prove a Mexican waiter I have never met in my life wrong.

His response was "Are you sure you want this bottle, this one next to it (three times more expensive) goes much better with lobster. You are getting lobster, right?"

"Yes, of course I am getting lobster," I said.

Apparently I was getting lobster.

I was now getting pissed, so I added "I am very familiar with this bottle (I wasn't) because after I received my fourth certification in education and my Master's degree in New Media Journalism, I decided to get trained as a sommelier. That is a wine expert in case you didn't know."

Still unimpressed, he walked away.

Proud that I stood up for myself, I began taking actual notes, basically all of which revolved around how much I hated this man.

He returned about twenty minutes later with my wine, showed me the bottle without speaking to me, and cranked it open (quite impressively I begrudgingly admit.)

I took a sip and while I wanted to say "It doesn't taste expensive enough, get me something even pricier," I said "This is just fine."

And he responded with "Yes, it is my favorite wine on the menu."

To which I replied, "Well then why did you try to convince me to not order it?"

He stared at me for a few seconds and then said "What else would you like besides the open faced lobster?"

Huh, I thought.

I didn't even know that is what I ordered, and I sure as shit didn't know I was expected to order something else, so in a panic I opened the menu and pointed to the first thing I saw.

"You want that first?" he said, "Before the lobster?"

"Sure," I said, confidently.

At this point, this man and I hated each other with a fiery passion. The couple next to me even said "Wow," to me when the waiter walked away.

I simply shrugged my shoulders and said "Gosh, does he hate me or what?" and began pouring myself some wine.

A few minutes later my "appetizer" arrived, which was basically a full fledged scallop meal big enough for me to eat for dinner, lunch the next day, and dinner again the following night.

Before I could even take a bite, the waiter turned around, approached the couple near me and said "Would you like to charge the meal to your room?"

Shocked at what I was hearing because I was told otherwise, I called the man over and said "You told me that I could only pay in cash, and you just asked them if they wanted to charge it to their room?"

"*You* have to pay in cash," the man said.

Then, for the first time in my entire life, I said something that I never thought would come out of my mouth…

"I would like to speak to your manager," I calmly requested.

Unphased, he said, "Follow me."

So I grabbed my glass of wine, and followed this horribly mean man to the lobby of the restaurant and explained exactly what my experience at the restaurant had been so far.

I told the manager I was a travel writer and have traveled around the world and have never been treated the way this man was treating me.

The manager calmly asked for my name, and assured me that this was very unlike the waiter. He typically is one of the best waiters they have.

"Well then I wouldn't want to see what the other ones are like," I said under my breath.

"What is your room number, sir. We can charge your meal to the room."

"Thank you," I said, before confidently saying "83401A."

The manager and another employee were now looking up my information to make sure I was who I said I was.

"What is your last name again, sir."

"Jacobson," I answered.

"This is not a room number, sir."

"Oh, maybe it is 84301A," I said, apologizing.

"No sir, that is not it either."

Fuck, I thought, I literally could not look any more suspicious at the moment, and I have absolutely no clue what my room number is.

Me: "83401B?"

Them: "Nope."

Me: "85304A?"

Them: "Nope!"

This went on and on until they had to eventually call the head office of the resort to have someone deal with the criminal that was trying to steal wine and a lobster dinner under the rouse of a "travel writer."

After nearly a half hour the main office finally figured out my room number and allowed the restaurant to charge my meal to their room. All this while happy couples were entering and exiting the restaurant problem free, with full bellies and big smiles across their faces.

And perhaps most tragic, all while my waiter was standing against the wall, arms crossed, with a shit-eating grin on his face.

Before I went back to my table, I said to the manager, loud enough for my waiter and whoever else was around to hear, "I WILL NOT BE GIVING HIM A TIP," to which the manager said "that is fine, Mr. Yacobson."

"It's Jacobson," I said, like a bratty child.

I scarfed down the rest of my meal and bottle of wine and left, already writing a seething, strongly worded email to the head of the resort in my mind.

I, however, am typically not one to hold grudges, and by the time I found my room the idea of writing an email seemed like too much work for me, so I walked into the pool, said hello to whoever else was swimming, and went to bed.

The next morning as I was walking down the long walkway to the beach, there was a man walking towards me.

With each step I became more and more certain that it was my waiter from the previous night. This was my chance…

I was going to tell him how mean he was, and how I am going to leave the worst review of all time for him. I was going to tell him that it was the worst service I have ever received in my entire life, and he owes me an apology for the way he treated me.

However, when he got right in front of me, before I could say a word he said "Hola, amigo."

My response:

"Hello, my friend. Have a good day at work!" and trudged along straight to the beach.

For a long time it was a complete mystery as to why that waiter was so put off by me that night at The Grand Riviera Princess Resort in Playa del Carmen, Mexico, but after months of processing the ordeal, I have since come to the conclusion that my waiter had a very close relative that was also employed at The Grand Princess Resort. I am not sure of the relation, maybe a father, grandfather, or great uncle. But I decided it was a man that goes by the name of Jose. Also known as The Greatest Security Guard of All Time.

28. Belize - Low Budget Death By Lionfish

Caye Caulker is a beautiful, small Caribbean island off the coast of Belize. I planned to simply stay on the island for my low budget Belize days and then move on to a new island, or to mainland Belize.

However, minutes after I stepped foot on the island, I decided I wanted to extend my time there and instead of switching locations, would do the full twelve days on Caye Caulker. I would still treat this as any other "Venture Twelve" experience by spending four days on a low budget, four on a moderate budget, and four on a luxury budget, but I would be doing so on the tiny island that was only five miles from north to south, and less than a mile long east to west.

There was no denying, I was about to get to know this island real well.

My first day I walked around the entire island to get the feel of it. The best part about living on an island so small is that, while it technically isn't impossible to get lost, it is very difficult to do.

One thing I noticed while making my rounds is that nearly every restaurant had huge chalkboard signs outside their place that said "Lionfish Special."

Upon talking to a few locals, I learned that the influx of lionfish is a huge problem in Belize. In the Caribbean, lionfish have no natural predators, breed at an alarming rate (a single female lionfish can lay up to 2 million eggs,) and are feeding on key species. They are posing a very serious threat to the health of the reefs in Belize, which would greatly impact their tourism.

So the Belize Lionfish Project was born and their main objective is to solve the lionfish problem by overfishing them and then eating them.

Naturally, I wanted to help the wonderful people of Belize out, so I decided that for at least my low budget days, I would eat lionfish every night in Caye Caulker. The first night went off without a hitch and the fish tasted delicious and fresh, and best of all, was extraordinarily cheap. The only hiccup was that the bones in the lionfish are so small, and the lighting was not too great in most restaurants, so you have to be very careful to not choke to death.

It takes approximately three million of the slowest chews imaginable in order for you to successfully eat a lionfish. But I was becoming an expert.

Filled to the brim with lionfish, I awoke the third morning at my low budget accommodation and was pleasantly surprised to see that a new guest had arrived. She, too, was a solo traveler, and from the looks of it, a writer as well. She sat at breakfast and wrote, while I sat at breakfast and wrote.

Then I saw her again at lunch, writing, which made me feel guilty for not writing, so I began writing as well.

She was so focused on her writing that I didn't want to interrupt her flow, so I kept to myself and never introduced myself.

On my fourth night on the island, I went to the same restaurant that I went every night for dinner. It was right next to my hotel, had an ocean front view, and delicious, cheap lionfish.

I saw the same girl sitting alone, and was about to sit next to her when I realized there were no chairs at her table (sharing of tables is common at the restaurant,) and sat about three tables down.

She ordered her lionfish, then I ordered my lionfish and both of ours came out nearly at the same time.

I took my very first bite and immediately started choking on a bone. So I did what any other normal person would do in that situation… I calmly got up, leaving my laptop, wallet and journal behind, and walked back to my hotel while muffling my choking sounds.

I would rather choke to death, alone in my hotel room in Belize than make a scene in front of this beautiful, mature, woman that clearly had her shit together way more than I did. So I made a gametime decision, and left to go die in my room.

Somehow by the grace of God, I managed to cough the bone up. I did my best to compose myself before walking back to the restaurant like nothing ever happened, and my plan worked. Not a single person noticed that the reason I left was because I had a lionfish bone lodged in my throat and I didn't want to die in front of them and ruin their fun time in Belize. Or if they did notice, nobody seemed to care.

When I returned, I ate the vegetables that were on my plate and pushed the lionfish around to make it look like I ate a large portion of it. As I was doing my best to force myself to eat my veggies (not sure if you have ever experienced it, but it is pretty traumatizing almost choking to death on a fishbone, so needless to say, I kind of lost my appetite) when I heard someone choking in the corner.

Sure enough, it was the hot solo traveler. She waved off the servers' and patrons' demands to help her dislodge the bone, giving the "thumbs up" when anyone approached her with the universal sign for choking. But for about ten minutes she was coughing and hacking away; and I know she didn't want or mean to, but she was making about as big of a scene as one could possibly make.

She was doing exactly what I was doing twenty minutes prior, just in the privacy of my own room. My eyes were watering (hers were too,) things were dripping out of my nose (same thing was happening to her), my face was bright red (she looked like beet.)

Welp, she is definitely choking on a lionfish bone, I know that look when I see it, I said to myself, diagnosing her on the spot.

I did my best to not look at her because I know she must have been mortified.

So I would take quick glances every minute or so, just to make sure she was still alive, once or twice accidentally making eye contact.

After she finally got her breath back, she immediately asked for the bill, while still coughing all over the place periodically.

She paid her bill and as she gathered her belongings and walked by me, I wanted to look as occupied as I possibly could so that I didn't have to risk making eye contact with her again. I was pretending I had no idea what the hell was going on, and didn't even hear all the commotion. I have never pretended to look so damn busy in all my life.

But just to be safe, I took a gigantic gulp of beer while she was walking by.

The problem was that I was so preoccupied at making sure we didn't make eye contact that I must have forgotten how to drink, and my entire gulp of warm beer went right down the wrong pipe.

I immediately started coughing and choking like an idiot, but this time there was no time to run to my room. People now started to run to me, and in between breaths, whenever I could get one, I said "Cerveza, not a bone," to anyone that was looking at me. Once everyone realized that there was nothing that anyone needed to dislodge from my throat, like they needed to do to the girl a few minutes prior, they left me alone and let me choke in peace.

White people, is what I imagined the entire restaurant was thinking about the two of us, as I was still choking. This made me laugh, which in turn, made me choke even harder.

Once I was able to breathe again, I immediately felt awful for the poor girl who almost choked to death right in front of everyone, and right as she was leaving she heard me choking.

All I could think about is that she must have thought I was mimicking or mocking her and the whole place was laughing at her expense.

I never saw her at breakfast, or ever again after that incident. I wanted so badly to see her and explain to her that I really was choking on beer, and she shouldn't be embarrassed about almost dying while eating a lionfish because I almost died twice during that same meal. I just had a better way of hiding it.

The first time, at least.

29. Belize
Moderate Budget
Death By Stingray

After my few days of living on Caye Caulker on a low budget, and all the lionfish I could possibly consume, not that I would ever attempt to eat one again after seeing my life flash before my eyes in the last chapter, it was time for me to spring into Caye Caulker action and step up my game on the Belizean island.

I packed up my belongings, checked out of my low budget accommodations (it was a dorm room with six bunk beds that I had all to myself) and walked two minutes to my next home; a moderately priced hotel with beach access, and a small, cozy bedroom and bathroom.

For the first few days of moderate Caye Caulker living, life wasn't exceptionally different other than the fact that I was able to be a little more loose with my money to spend on fancier drinks, meals other than "lionfish specials," and most importantly, leisure and activities.

I rented snorkel gear to use in the beach waters on which my hotel was located. I rented a golf cart for a day to take me to parts of the island I didn't want to walk to. And most memorable of all, I decided to fork up the money for a once in a lifetime experience of participating in the most popular activity in Caye Caulker; swimming with sharks and stingrays.

To many people this may seem like a crazy and dangerous thing to do. But if you mention your hesitation to local Caye

Caulkers, you will be looked at as if you are the most pathetic letdown that has ever stepped foot on their beautiful island.

I had no choice, in order to get the full Caye Caulker experience I had to man up and swim with killer animals.

I know of many places around the world that offer "swimming with the sharks" activities as in the type of adventure where you, the human, are lowered into the ocean in a cage, safely enclosed by metal bars and attached to a rope which would pull you out should anything go wrong.

So when I first stepped on the boat, my eyes were wandering all over the place looking for the cage we would be lowered in, but couldn't spot one.

As the boat started loading up with passengers (about 20 of us in all) our Belizean guides introduced themselves to us. I asked my fellow adventurers if they knew where the cage was, only to get very strange glances as a response. Glances that implied, *Who is in charge of this guy?* and *Why is he asking me about a cage?*

Earlier in the morning, at the office in which I purchased the ticket for the experience, the worker repeatedly reminded me of all the things I would need to bring with me for the day… a towel, bathing suit, camera, and most importantly, sunscreen and bottles of water. She handed me my ticket and told me to report back in an hour, and gave me time to gather my items from my room, or make any necessary purchases before the boat departed.

I already had a bathing suit on and I brought a bottle of water with me because it was about 110 degrees and I didn't want to drop dead of dehydration before I had the chance to be eaten by sharks. I also had my camera with me because it stayed by my side for an entire year. Three out of five… *not too bad,* I thought to myself. The towel, and the sunscreen were extras in my mind.

Back on the boat, it was approaching 9:30 a.m. by the time all the pleasantries and instructions were out of the way, and we began to take off into the middle of the ocean at mock 10 speed. My hat managed to stay on my head for approximately 12 seconds before flying off into the ocean and becoming fish food, while I was still busy unsuccessfully looking all around for the damn cage in which we would be lowered.

Our group began to chat with one another in all of our broken languages. Australians, Germans, Italians, and even some of our neighbors to the north, the Canadians were participating in the adventure.

As the passengers all began applying their sunscreen, the girl next to me noticed I had none and offered me hers. I politely refused, and her boyfriend said, "You're probably going to need it bro, we did this two years ago and I got the shit burnt out of me.

I reluctantly said "Just a dabble," and the kind girl placed a small squeeze on the tip on my finger, which was all I was offering up.

I placed the sunscreen on my nose, and blended it in to make sure I wasn't sitting there making new friends with big blobs of sunscreen all over the crevices of my nose.

"All blended in?" I asked the girl.

Laughing at my lightning fast application of sunscreen she said, sarcastically, "You're good to go, mate."

We were cruising through the waters, making our way to snorkel in one of the most legendary coral reefs in the world, the Belize Barrier Reef. About ten minutes after the boat took off, we stopped in the middle of the ocean and the captain shut off the motor.

The instructors separated us into four groups of five and we were told we were free to dive into the water with our snorkel gear and explore the Belize Barrier Reef. They directed us to stay relatively close together so we didn't get lost.

But, wait, aren't there sharks here? I asked my instructor, trying to hide the panic in my voice.

"No sharks or stingrays here, sir. You can relax," said the instructor.

Putting every ounce of trust in the man, I grabbed my snorkel gear and GoPro and jumped off the boat into the water.

The reefs were as majestic as all the guidebooks said they would be. Gorgeous, colorful reefs were everywhere you looked, full of life and vibrancy. Little fish were appearing and disappearing into the tiny crevices of the reefs, only to return moments later with equally colorful fish friends.

We had a full thirty minutes to explore the reefs on our own. It was like I was suddenly thrown into a live action role in *The Little Mermaid*, swimming peacefully through reefs, half expecting Ariel herself to appear at any moment.

After our half hour was up, we all gathered on the boat, eager to share our experiences and more importantly, GoPro photos with each other, as the instructors explained to us that we were heading off to the main event… swimming with the sharks and stingrays.

I settled in, expecting a lengthy boat ride until we reached the area where we would get into the water with the sharks (in a cage.) But much to my surprise the boat stopped just five minutes from where we were snorkeling in the reef.

Wait… there will be sharks and stingrays HERE, but there were none just five minutes away? I thought to myself, feeling duped.

The Instructors explained to us how it would work…

They took out a bucket of chum and passed it around for all of us to see. They explained that they would drop the chum into the water, which would attract the sharks and stingrays to the boat. Then, we would get in and swim with them. The only rule, try to remain quiet… no yelling to each other, or back to the guides on the boat, as it would likely frighten the animals away and ruin the experience.

"In a cage, right?" I asked, just assuming he left that part out of the instructions.

"No cage, you just swim with them," he said, throwing the chum into the water.

Within seconds I saw not just one or two, but dozens of sharks approaching the boat, and feverishly attacking the chum.

I then watched as one by one my fellow passengers jumped off the boat and frolicked in the water as even more sharks came in.

Without second guessing myself, I too, jumped in, scared out of my mind.

I whipped out my GoPro and got as close to the sharks as my fear-filled body would allow me, snapping some impressive pictures along the way, and eventually almost forgetting that these were killer animals.

Suddenly, as I was getting some video footage of the sharks, I felt someone smash into me. I apologized *underwater(!)* and with a snorkel in my mouth(!), as if the person I was apologizing to could understand what I was saying.

But when I looked over to see which of my boatmates I smashed into, I was staring into the eyes of an enormous stingray, swimming right beside me.

I let out a little "Yelp" before I realized the cardinal rule: no screaming.

I ripped off my snorkel gear and came above the water to calm myself down and figure out the path of least resistance to get back to the boat. For some reason, the sharks didn't scare me as much as the stingrays. I wasn't about to pull a Steve Irwin in Belize, and I felt as though I already got my money's worth.

As I was above water, trying to get an aerial view to scan my surroundings, I felt something jump on my back. Again, thinking it was a fellow passenger, I turned around as a stingray popped out of the water and jumped right on top of me.

Without thinking, I released such a blood curdling scream that if I was auditioning for the role of Drew Barrymore's character in the 1996 horror movie *Scream*, I am confident I would have gotten the part over her. I screamed out of the water, then went under the water to get the stingray away from me, and continued my record breaking shriek.

And as quickly as the sharks and stingrays appeared, they disappeared; terrified of the noise that came out of my mouth.

I swam faster than Michael Phelps back to the boat, hopped on, and explained to the few passengers that had already chickened out what happened. They shared that the same thing happened to them earlier, but they didn't want to scream, so they came back on the boat.

You know who else came back on the boat shortly after… EVERYBODY else. You know why? Because there was nothing left to look at besides a few random stingrays that I didn't happen to scare away.

If our boat was playing *Survivor* on the way home, I would have been the odds on favorite to be the first person voted out because I essentially ruined the experience for all aboard.

We did make one more stop that day as a group; a seahorse farm, where we got the opportunity to see real seahorses up close and personal. Selflessly, I chose[4] to stay in the very back of the group so as to not ruin another once-in-a-lifetime experience for everyone else.

---

[4] Was kindly asked to stay in the back by the instructors and my fellow passengers.

30. Belize - Luxury Budget Death By Hell's Itch

Many people have horror stories about things going terribly wrong while traveling or on a vacation. While I had certainly experienced my fair share of unfortunate situations while traveling for the past nine months, nothing could come close to being categorized as a true "horror story."

That is until my final days spent in Caye Caulker, Belize luxury.

After my day of swimming with the sharks and stingrays, I was to spend the final four days of my time in Caye Caulker on an all-out luxury budget. I had plans to dine in some of their most talked about restaurants, and booked a helicopter excursion to fly over the illustrious Great Blue Hole, a gigantic marine sinkhole that was explored by Jacques Cousteau.

However, none of this happened during my stay in Caye Caulker luxury.

Remember back to when the ticket agent for my swimming and stingray tour mentioned the items I would need for the adventure?

Bathing suit, towel, water, camera and sunscreen?

If you recall, I opted against the sunscreen and the only lotion I applied was a dabble to my nose when prompted by another passenger.

Around the time I was checking into my luxury hotel on the beach, I started getting signs of an intense, yet tolerable itch on my back. I chalked it up to a bit of a sunburn, and carried on with the check-in process.

I was delighted when I walked into my beautiful oceanfront bedroom, complete with a living area, kitchen, and luxurious bathroom.

Not long after I was settled in though, I realized the itch was intensifying and felt more like shards of glass, rather than a pesky itch. The more I tried not to focus on it, the worse it became.

I walked down the road to the nearest store and purchased a soothing cream that was meant to treat sunburn irritation, and headed back to my room.

If you have ever tried to apply a lotion to your own back, you can imagine what the scene was like in my hotel room as I frantically tried spreading the lotion onto every inch.

I never experienced a sunburn, or general pain like what I was experiencing in Caye Caulker "luxury."

Realizing that this wasn't just a regular sunburn, I began frantically searching the internet for what could possibly be wrong with me, and stumbled upon something called "Hell's itch," also commonly known as "The Devil's itch," "Fire ant itch," or even "Suicide itch," which based on the limited research that has been conducted on the condition, is estimated to have impacted about five percent of the world's population.

I know what you're thinking… you've had a sunburn before, and can imagine how bad my back burned.

I am here to unequivocally tell you that a sunburn and Hell's itch are two very different things, and unless you are one of the five percent of the population that has experienced it, you can not begin to imagine the pain.

In my frantic research to figure out what the hell was going on with me (there are no hospitals on Caye Caulker,) I stumbled upon an article by Dr. Cory Stewart, now an orthopedic surgeon at the University of Chicago. He described the itch as a "Debilitating, madness-inducing itch that has brought US Marines to their knees and has trumped the pain of childbirth for mothers."

Dr. Martin Steinhoff, one of the world's leading sunburn researchers said he has "Encountered many patients in the throes of Hell's itch," and has reported them saying "It is the worst itch imaginable and has left them pretty much dysfunctional. For upward of two days, patients are completely consumed by the itch, unable to work or to even think straight."

There is no cure except time, and lotions and creams not only are ineffective, but often make things even worse.

The only known temporary relief, based on the "Hell's itch" online community of unfortunate people that have experienced it, is ironically, scalding hot showers. And Benadryl.

Dr. Steinhoff has said that a boiling hot shower "Activates the skin's pain nerves, shutting down the itch. In more severe cases of chronic itch, the same logic has even prompted sufferers to take lighters to their skin." Even adding "It can be as severe as chronic pain. It can lead to suicide, to sleep deprivation, to depression, it can lead to aggressiveness."

I thought it was a bit anti-climatic starting out with "It can lead to suicide," and ending with "It can lead to agressiveness," but I get the point, Dr. Steinhoff.

If you search for Youtube videos about people experiencing Hell's itch you can see first hand the torture they are going through, only to hear their friends and family members mocking them in the background and calling them "wimps," or "drama queens."

So I was beyond grateful to be all alone during my time in hell.

After taking in all the advice I could find online, I knew that the only way I would get through the trauma was to take scalding hot showers and come as close to overdosing on Benadryl as a human could.

So shortly after checking into my luxury hotel, I was taking the hottest shower I could tolerate, and the relief instantly kicked in. I could finally think straight. The hot shower allowed me to think of a plan of action…

I would stay in the shower under the scorching water for as long as I could stand it. Then, during my brief period of relief I would run to the store, buy as much Benadryl as I could find, and get right back in the shower.

I got out of the shower and threw on a bathing suit without drying off because the thought of a towel touching my back was incomprehensible. I grabbed my wallet and ran to the store. Luckily they had plenty of Benadryl, so I bought it all. I knew I had a limited amount of time before the pain kicked in again, so I walked up and down my road adjacent to the beach to purchase anything I may need to spend the next few days in the shower.

I got a few essentials such as crackers and chips. The pain was so intense I couldn't even dream of eating or ever having an appetite again.

Then I stopped at the beach bar outside of my hotel, ordered a margarita, which I drank in three sips, and asked for another margarita to-go.

I figured if I was buzzed, the pain would be a bit more manageable.

I got back to my room just in time for the pain to become excruciating again, grabbed my to-go margarita and returned to the hot shower, not even bothering to take off my bathing suit this time.

After the next hour-long shower, I repeated the process. Still unable to use a towel to dry off, I ran out of my room, soaking wet, walked to the bar, downed a margarita, and ordered another one to go.

One Youtuber described the pain of "Hell's itch" as getting a full back tattoo while the tattoo artist randomly sticks the needle in real deep every once in a while.

Another describes the pain as thousands of red ants attacking your back at once, and every now and then one of the red ants will eat its way into your body and start attacking from the inside.

I can assure you they are not exaggerating.

The first two nights I ended up sleeping in the shower… turning the boiling water on every hour or so to relieve the pain.

Each morning I would begin the same routine of going to the beach bar, ordering a margarita, and taking one to-go for me to sip on while in the shower.

With my "Do Not Disturb" sign on my door for four days straight, I can not be sure what the workers must have thought about what the hell I was doing in my room and with all those margaritas, but at that point I didn't care.

It wasn't until my final day in Caye Caulker that I was able to function as a normal human being again. As I walked by the beach bar with all my bags, the bartender that had served me no less than 24 margaritas in a three day span yelled to me, "No margarita today, sir?"

I was leaving the country and heading to Costa Rica to spend a month-long "break" from the *Venture Twelve* project and get some writing done in solitude. So I said, "No margarita today, sir, but here, this is for you," and handed him all of my leftover Belizean money that I didn't get to spend during my stay in luxury.

All I can hope is that he didn't use the money to go on a swimming with sharks and stingrays tour. Or at least if he did, he was smart enough to use sunscreen.

31. Panama - Low Budget Good DryDay

In many parts of the world, there are designated "dry days" that are typically observed on religious holidays. These are specific days in which the sale of alcohol is not permitted under any circumstance until the clock ticks midnight.

I arrived in Panama City two days before Easter Sunday, known to most of the world as Good Friday… or what I now refer to as "Not-So-Good-Dryday."

Not only did I just get done spending a planned month in solitude in the jungles of Costa Rica to work on my writing, but this was also a special day because it signaled the return of Erin, who decided to come visit me again on the adventure since she enjoyed her time so very much in Morocco and Eastern Europe with me.

This would be the first time I had seen anyone I knew from home in over four months. Her arrival was the cause for some much needed celebration as we began our journey in Panama, and prepared and planned for our venture to Colombia.

With her arriving by plane from the States and me arriving by bus from Costa Rica, it was serendipitous when we both walked into our hostel within minutes of each other.

After a warm embrace and some brief catching up, we walked up to the reception desk and got the keys to our hostel room, which we would share with six strangers, likely to be much younger than us.

While spending ⅓ of the year traveling around the world on a low budget, I had grown accustomed to staying at hostels, and was rarely, if ever, turned off by the idea of sleeping in a room with complete strangers.

For the most part, no matter how many beds are in the hostel room, the room is almost always empty except at night. People do not get hostel rooms in order to waste the day away in their twin or bunk bed.

Instead, they take advantage of the money they are saving by not getting an expensive hotel room and are out exploring the city in which they are temporarily residing.

And if they are not out galavanting around the city, they can most likely be found in one of the hostel's common areas, such as the indoor or outdoor lounge, the kitchen and dining area, or more often than not, the bar.

Hostel bars are quite possibly my favorite places in the world for many reasons. First, while typically offering a limited variety of options, whatever they are selling is as cheap as you will find anywhere else in the city. Large beers often go for the equivalent of a dollar or two, hard alcohol just a bit more.

But way more importantly, is the fact that there is nowhere on Earth that is easier to make friends from all over the world. Many people staying at hostels are solo travelers from other countries, if not, a duo traveling together.

Everyone is ready to mingle with new people, and eager to learn all about their new roommates, if only for the night.

So at 3:00 p.m. when Erin and I walked into our hostel room that slept eight, and found only three empty beds, we were a bit perplexed. The other five beds had twenty-somethings from all over the world occupying them. I did not see any of their faces, nor did they care to look up at ours to catch a glimpse of their new roomies. One was sleeping, one was reading, and the other three had their eyes glued to their cell phones, presumably getting the scoop on what was happening in the lives of their loved ones so many miles away.

It is not wildly uncommon to see one or two people taking midday naps in hostel rooms, but to have nearly the entire room filled in peak exploration hours was virtually unheard of.

We deposited our bags onto two of the open beds, officially claiming them as ours, and gave a silent nod to each other implying we needed to get the hell out of the awkward room as soon as possible.

Once outside the room we decided to go for a quick tour of our enormous hostel, which had a gym, a movie theater, a large kitchen, and a restaurant and bar area. On the rooftop was an inground swimming pool, and a hot tub big enough to fit approximately twenty people.

Also on the rooftop were two more bars, and a view of Panama City that by itself, was worth the $6 a night that we were paying to stay there.

We decided that rather than rushing out and exploring the city in the midday heat, we would relax and take in the views of the city from the top of our ridiculously nice hostel.

The pool was filled with young, beautiful travelers whose accents stretched from Australian, British, and Canadian, to a mixture of German/English, French/English, Italian/English and finally to full-on Russian with a few English proper nouns tossed in.

For example, we heard from the lounge chairs by the entrance a conversation in Russian that went like this...

"Я не могу поверить, что они не обслуживают **BUDWEISER** сегодня из-за глупого правила сухого дня."

"Если бы не это правило сухого дня, у нас сейчас было бы 5 **Pina ColadaS**."

I am aware that much of the Russian language sounds very angry even if they're talking about cute little puppies and sweet little old ladies, but these Russians *really* didn't sound happy about whatever they were talking about. All I knew was that it had to do with Budweiser and Pina Coladas. Also, I am 100% certain I heard the word "водка" or "vodka" no less than 45 times in the 30 seconds I was standing next to them.

And while the pool was full of hostel-goers, none of them looked extraordinarily happy. Some, I admit, even looked downright miserable.

As usual Erin and I walked straight up to the bar, plopped our asses down on the bar stools and waited for the Australian, surfer dude bartender to come over and take our order.

"Wow. What a lame bunch of hostel-goers, I have never seen anything quite like it," I said to Erin.

"In all the hostels I have stayed in, this is by far the most depressed looking bunch of people I have ever seen," replied Erin.

Oh well, I thought, *if there is one thing Erin and I do not need to have a good time, it's other people.*

"I guess it is a good thing," I said out loud to Erin, "the last thing we need are bad influences. Maybe it's good this is a lame bunch. I may be able to get some writing done, and you may even be able to get some work done," I tried to add, before both of us started laughing hysterically at the idea of such a ridiculous thought.

Now, the entire rooftop of beautiful, miserable, half-naked, co-ed foreigners were staring at us, the two old, loud, Americans that had the audacity to laugh and have a good time.

"Shhh," I whispered to Erin, we don't want to distract the buzzkills from their collective mourning session.

One positive thing that did happen though, is our outburst of laughter caught the attention of the bartender, who promptly came over to us and apologized for not seeing us sooner.

"How may I help you mates?" said the young Australian hippy with the biggest, bluest eyes I have ever seen in my life. He was grinning from ear to ear, and could not be any happier to be working. I am assuming he had made it as far as Panama before his money ran out, and this was his first gig since leaving Australia, God knows how long ago, where he could finally make a few bucks a day to continue his quest of catching a wave in every country in the world.

"Hey mate," I said back to him, not sounding anywhere close to as cool as when he said it. This, in turn, made Erin flash me a look that said "if you ever talk like that again, I am flying home and will never be associated with you again for the rest of our lives."

I simply rolled my eyes and said "Shut up," before she even had the chance to open her mouth and make fun of me.

"Two large beers and two shots of whatever you recommend," I said, excited as hell to finally be able to cheers with Erin once more and toast to us finding good fortune in Panama and Colombia.

"Ohhhhhhhhhhhh, sorry mate. You must not have heard that it is Good Friday, broski. It is a dry day here. No alcohol sales today. Bummer, I know," said the simpleminded, handsome, presumably homeless surfer.

"WHATTTTT. None at all? Anywhere?" Erin and I screamed back in unison, as I immediately had flashbacks to eight months prior in New Delhi, India where this same nightmare took place.

"Crikey. Sorry mates, none at all," he replied, his huge smile slowly fading from his face. "It would be gnarly if I could sneak you a few coldies, but I can't. Sorry, mates," he said, sounding just as heartbroken as we were.

We looked at each other, then behind us at all the hostel guests who were still staring at us, all shaking their heads in sadness, as if to say "why the fuck do you idiots think we are just chilling out over here, and not drinking beers?"

Even the Russians were looking at us, and although we did not speak the same language, we didn't need to. We felt each other's pain.

Defeated, we thanked the Australian dude and made our way to the lounge chairs to join our depressed comrades.

"Cheer up, amigos, the people at the front desk told us that they would open the bar at 8:00 pm, even though they are not supposed to until midnight," said a Spanish guy we later came to find out was going to the same cities, on the same days, in Colombia that we were going to the following week."

We watched as one by one newbies came up to the rooftop and did the exact same thing we did. I am not sure why, but none of us would stop them. Perhaps we wanted them to feel the same joy and excitement that we all felt when seeing the rooftop for the first time, only to have the crushing blow of defeat when finding out all the bars in the city were closed. We subconsciously must have thought this would possibly bond us and connect us by being able to feel each other's sorrow.

The group got bigger and bigger as the evening went on. I would estimate that over 30 countries were represented on that rooftop that day. All of us wallowing in the same sadness. It didn't matter where we were from, we all felt the same.

The closer it got to 8:00 p.m. the more lively the group became. By 7:30 p.m. we were all long lost friends that knew everything about each other; our travels, our plans, our hopes, our dreams and our life goals. We were teaching each other important words and puns from our own respected languages, and we were all truly enveloped in each other's stories.

At 8:00 p.m. we all ran up to the bar. The Australian bartender yelled to all of us at once "Mates, I know you heard that we may open at eight, but it is a royal bummer to tell you that we can't do that and you have to wait until midnight."

At this point many people retreated to their room, making plans to reconvene in four hours as we showered, dressed in our evening attire and did whatever else we needed to do in order to avoid the depressing, desolate bar and the naked bar stools that sat, waiting to be occupied.

Erin and I personally promised every single person on that rooftop we would join the twenty-somethings at midnight and, while I can't be certain, we more than likely promised each and every one of them we would buy them a round.

When we got in the room, we saw it was entirely filled with foreigners in their own beds, but now, instead of thinking of them as lame and buzzkills, we knew they were just sad about the "Not-So-Good-Dry Day" we found ourselves experiencing. They were likely just resting up for the rooftop bar to open. Neither myself or Erin said a single word to any of them, nor did we ever end up catching even a glimpse of any of their faces.

"Midnight is very late," I whispered to Erin.

"I am ready for bed right now," she confessed.

"Me too," I said sadly.

I fell asleep before I could even say my prayers, thanking God for all the great people I met from around the world and being able to have such an immediate connection and bond with them; for being able to hear stories of their lives that were so similar to mine in so many ways, yet so incredibly different from mine in an equal amount of ways.

Hours later I was awoken by the thunderous roar of celebration as I whispered to Erin, "It must be midnight. I am so happy for all our friends. Such fun they must be having, being young and so full of energy."

But she didn't respond. She was still fast asleep. Sleeping so hard that not even the screams of happiness from representatives from every country in the entire world, and every animal on all of Noah's Ark could have awoken her.

Before I fell back asleep I opened up my laptop and did a Google search for "Are bars in Panama City…"

And before I could even finish asking my question, Google knew what I was going to ask.

"Are bars in Panama City open on Holy Saturday," was the first suggested phrase that popped up.

I can not be certain, of course, but I imagined that the six roommates that were sleeping in my room typed in that exact same phrase before me, and that is how Google knew what I was going to say.

It turns out they would be open the next day. And even on Easter Sunday.

I shut my computer, closed my eyes, and smiled. Then I thanked God for the coolest six roommates that anyone could ever ask for.

32. Panama
Moderate Budget
The Sole Survivor

In March of 2000, sixteen American strangers were gathered and marooned on Pulau Tiga, an island off the western coast of Sabah, Malaysia. The object of the game they volunteered for was simple; they would live there for 39 days, trying to survive not only the elements on the island, but also, survive each other.

Survivor is born.

I have been addicted to any type of elimination games, or tournaments for as long as I can remember, a fact which can easily be proven by listing my favorite things growing up as a child...

WWF Battle Royals

This is the semi-annual event in which twenty or so professional wrestlers would enter the ring at the same time. The object being to try and throw all the other men over the ropes and out of the ring, thus getting eliminated, until only one man remained and became the Battle Royal champion. Nothing, in the entire world, made eight-year old Ryan happier than a Battle Royal Saturday night event.

The Miss USA/America pageants

51 of the most beautiful women from all over the country would compete in various rounds of competition; swimsuit, evening gown, talent, question and answer, etc. Each round multiple women would be eliminated until only one woman remained, claiming the

title of Miss USA/America. 51 to 15 to 10 to 5...4...3...2...1. I am not sure what it says about me that I found so much joy as a child watching the hopes and dreams of 50 women get shattered on the biggest night of their lives, but I sure as hell loved it.

NCAA March Madness

This should not come as a shock, but the NCAA March Madness basketball tournament that begins with 64 teams and over the course of a few weeks eliminates 63 of them in heartbreaking, nail-biting losses that end many collegiate athletes careers, has always been, and will always be my favorite sporting event.

Dodgeball (the game)

I am willing to bet that there are people that have literally won the Powerball lottery that have reacted in a more calm, controlled manner than 12-year old Ryan would act when he discovered he was playing dodgeball in gym class. The object of the game: smash people with balls as hard as you can, thus eliminating participants one by one until one team has lost all of its members, making them the winner of gym class dodgeball.

So when I heard about the television show *Survivor*, an entire SEASON of a show solely dedicated to eliminating someone each episode by way of their peers voting them out until only one person was left, I was hooked.

At 8:00 p.m. on **Thursday, May 31st, 2000** the television screen in the basement of my parent's house went from the credits of *Jeopardy* to a two second blackout that seemed, at the time, like the longest two seconds of my life.

Then, suddenly an aerial shot of Borneo appeared, showing 16 castaways boarding a boat which would take them to their island, while the following words from host Jeff Probst gently filled our ears like a chorus of angels.

"From this tiny Malaysian fishing village, these sixteen Americans are beginning the adventure of a lifetime. They have volunteered to be marooned for thirty-nine days on mysterious Borneo. This is their story. This is *Survivor.*"

Even today, two decades after that moment, I still get the chills writing it.

So when Erin and I were in Panama City deciding where we would spend our moderate budget days, I all but insisted we head to the Pearl Islands, a chain of over 200 islands about 30 miles off the Pacific coast of Panama. The islands, which are accessible by an affordable ferry that doubles as a mini cruise through the archipelago, is the location for three seasons of my favorite television show, including two of the most legendary seasons of all time, *Survivor: Pearl Islands,* and *Survivor: All Stars.*

After researching whether or not we could legitimately spend four days in the Pearl Islands and not exceed our moderate budget, we were over the moon when we discovered how cheap it would be, and changed our intended plans of heading to the much more popular, touristy, and "Instagram worthy" San Blas Islands.

One of my biggest dreams of all time was about to come true: I was about to visit a *Survivor* island.

There was one issue though. Naturally, the show is filmed on the uninhabited islands of the archipelago, not the one in which the ferry will deposit you, Isla Contadora. But this was a problem for later: I would make it to the actual "*Survivor*" island if I had to swim there.

Today most visitors to Isla Contadora in the Pearl Islands come for either a day trip from Panama City or perhaps a one or two night stay due to the fact that there is relatively nothing to do on the island except relax. 40 years ago the island was virtually unknown to the vast majority of the world.

The island, however, gained notoriety back in 1979 when the Shah of Iran retreated there in exile.

After that, seeing as the island was deemed luxurious enough for the Shah of Iran to live, it became a luxurious getaway for the rich and famous. Still today about half of the tiny island is covered in multimillion dollar private condos and villas that would more than satisfy the needs of even the most elusive celebrities.

It is a tropical paradise in which you can cut yourself off from the rest of the world and live in complete isolation, as long as you have the means to pay for it. It is, without question, one of the best hidden gems of luxurious paradise.

Aside from the private villas and condos, the rest of the island is, as they say, "Where the other half live."

And by "Other half," I mean about 130 people.

At last check, the entire population of Isla Contadora was 250 people, nearly half of which are those multimillionaires that visit their mansions dangling so close to the ocean that it seems like a sneeze from a giraffe could knock the whole place into the water.

When your ferry arrives near the island, you are directed to exit the ferry and get into a smaller boat that will take you to shore.

Well, close to shore at least, then you are on your own to roll up your pants, secure your belongings, and jump into the knee-deep water and trudge up to the beach.

You will instantly be bombarded with locals looking to take you to where you need to go, or rent you a golf cart, or rent you a boat, or get you a room. Basically anything that you could want to do on the islands, you can make reservations before you exit the high tide line of the beach.

This could be a smidge overwhelming for the untrained traveler, so my recommendation is to wave them off and walk to the "center" of "town," which in this case is about a quarter mile walk up a hill, in which you will find yourself walking past a cafe (which also offers golf cart rentals,) three different restaurants, which you will be eating your breakfast, lunch and dinner with the same employees and same guests gathering at each meal, and the islands one "major" convenience store (which doubles as a restaurant, bar, and most importantly, hotel.)

This is where we would stay for the next four days. A one bedroom/bathroom costs us about $60 USD for four nights. We could walk downstairs and eat lunch for about $5. We could grab beers from the convenience store for about $2 each, and we could rent a golf cart to trot around the island for about $10 USD / day.

Scattered around the rest of the island are small huts which double as homes where locals reside while they are not tending to tourists. There is also a small area of the island with modest homes that seem as though they only have an occasional visitor, the remainder of the year, remain vacant.

While this isn't the actual island beach that the *Survivor* castaways lived, it did house most of the crew during the filming. As a result of the filming, Pearl Islands received a sum of money from CBS, which is obvious from the many vacated construction sites scattered throughout the island. However, it seems as though their eyes were bigger than their heads because there is no indication that construction will resume any time soon.

A bit of background... *Survivor Pearl Islands* and *Survivor All Stars* were seasons seven and eight respectively. This means they were filmed in 2004, approximately 15 years prior to our visit. Most of the island has long since forgotten about the filming and it is but a distant memory to them.

So there were a few, let's say, hiccups, that I had when trying to get to the bottom of where Johnny Fair Play told the epic lie that his grandmother died, where the Queen of *Survivor,* Sandra Diaz-Twine won her first million dollars, and where *Survivor* royalty, Boston Rob, and his wife Amber Brkich, met on the beach for the first time during *Survivor: All Stars.*

But don't think that I didn't do my research to figure it out on my own. I had more island maps, notes and printouts of important filming locations and tools than Inspector Gadget had materials for his investigations.

A compass. I had a fucking compass.

I spent the first day on the island studying maps while lying on a beach, and walking up and down the shore, pointing to each island I saw in the distance, then looking back at my map, and back at the island before confirming to Erin, "Yup. That must be Isla Saboga. That is absolutely where the Saboga tribe lived, and where many of the challenges took place."

Then I would go back to studying the map, saying, "OK, if Isla Saboga is there, THAT island (pointing far in the distance) must be Chapera Island, where the Chapera tribe got its name and other challenges took place."

This would carry on for hours…. "THERE! That has GOT to be Isla Mogo Mogo," I exclaimed, to nobody, seeing as even Erin was now completely and utterly disinterested and the only thing she was searching for was the nearest mojito stand.

Now, if only I could find this damn island with this gigantic rock where they filmed the All Stars Tribal Council. That would be almost too much excitement to handle, I kept saying to myself.

I was a cartographer, an explorer, and a detective all in one. I was both Lewis and Clarke. I was Christopher Colombus. I was Sherlock Holmes. I was Ferdinand Magellan. I was Amerigo Vespucci. I was Marco. Fucking. Polo.

I drew out my map of the islands, proud that I was able to research all of the facts on my own and plan my adventure for the next day when we would go on a private island hopping tour. But my joy would always fade into dismal gloom at my inability to find the damn beach where All Stars Tribal Council was filmed.

At Erin's insistence, she made me take a break and join her in the beautiful blue ocean that I had been searching into for hours, the way a child searches their home on Easter morning to be absolutely positive that there are no eggs left hidden to fill their basket.

I gave in to her request to join her in the ocean, I neatly folded my shirt and placed it on my towel. I put a bookmark in my journal, so I knew where to continue my quest for Tribal Council when I got out of my break in the ocean, and I put my phone, which I was also using for my sleuthing skills in our bag, which I placed up against the rock wall adjacent to where our towels had been.

Then, for the first time, I went swimming in the Pearl Islands. The water was the temperature of a boiling hot bath tub after you let it cool off for about ten minutes. It was perfect.

The waves were so big that the only thought that went through my head each time I was body surfing was *please don't break your neck, please don't break your neck, please don't break your neck...* and they were only getting bigger as our ocean frolic continued.

I kept yelling to Erin "Jeff Probst has probably SWAM in this water. My favorite male *Survivor* of all time, Andrew Savage, has definitely swam in THIS water."

Little old me. Just a guy from a small town in the smallest state. Actually swimming in the same ocean that JEFF PROBST probably swam in about 18 years ago, I thought out loud.

I was essentially star struck. By the ocean.

I was in a world of my own. Trying to remember every single episode of all three seasons, and trying to place this very spot of ocean in any scene that would allow me.

My daydream was only broken by the sound of Erin screaming "A ROCK WALL! HOLY SHIT! A ROCK WALL! IT'S THE BIG ROCK WALL YOU HAVE BEEN SCEARCHING FOR WHERE YOUR STUPID TRIBAL COUNCIL WAS FILMED!"

I turned to look at the shore where she was frantically pointing and my eyes began to bug out of my head. If you were looking at me you would visibly be able to see my brain trying to piece together all of the information I had gathered about where this All Star Tribal Council was filmed. It was like I was solving the world's greatest math problem, or being the first person to discover that the world was round.

I was the word EUREKA! personified.

"LET'S GO!" I screamed, as we both ran out of the water as fast as we could.

Of course, being 15 years later, the actual Tribal Council set was no longer there, but I knew, without a shadow of a doubt that the decaying, decrepit rock stairs that remained were absolutely, positively, the stairs climbed by my favorite *Survivor* players ever.

Without saying a word, Erin and I both knew what was in store for the next few hours, she would be subjected to operating a full-on photo shoot of me climbing up and down a million stairs pretending I was walking to and from Tribal Council.

"Now take one of me pretending I am sad because I think I am about to get voted out," I would yell, as she stood on the beach taking photos from every angle that I ordered.

"Now let's take a few of me being really happy, like I just voted out my biggest rival," I would demand.

"Now let's take a video."

"Now, how about a few still frames."

"Try some in black and white."

"Tell me to do something. Direct me. How do I look?" I would scream, all the while the rest of the people on the beach thinking I had extraordinarily special needs.

This went on for a long while, and to be perfectly honest, might still be going on today had we not been distracted by the screams of the lovely elderly couple that we had placed our belongings down next to hours ago.

"HELLO! You two! On the stairs taking pictures! Quick!!!!"

We looked over to see what all the commotion was about and who was being so rude as to disrupt my Tribal Council photo shoot only to see them racing for our belongings which were being washed away by the ocean.

During our photo shoot the tide kept coming in, until the point where one wave washed away all our belongings and took them back into the ocean.

I could see my fluorescent orange towel floating in the ocean, my shirt was completely missing. My journal, with all my important *Survivor* facts, along with all the maps to the filming locations, was still drifting in the shallow water, but nearly illegible.

Erin's sunglasses were gone, our bag filled mostly with all her belongings, and my phone was there, but drenched.

The elderly couple apologized for not being able to get to our belongings sooner.

"We feel so sorry. We should have been quicker," they kept repeating.

Erin assured them that we were so grateful they even told us, otherwise we would have never known and would have lost everything.

My response wasn't so sincere. Instead of thanking the couple for saving Erin's bag, which was holding all of our money, the first words out of my mouth were… "Did you know this is where they filmed *Survivor All Stars* Tribal Council back in 2004?"

The couple stared at me in confusion.

"Thank you again," Erin said, physically pulling my arm and tearing me away from blankly staring at the rock wall. "You have a big day of island hopping to filming locations tomorrow. You need to go home, make sure you get a brand new photo card in your camera, and get a good night's rest."

33. Panama - Luxury Budget (In Colombia) Cartagena's Game of Thrones

Time is running out on my year-long venture around the world, so in order to experience as many different cultures and visit as many countries as possible, Erin and I decided to depart Panama after a week and spend our days of luxury in Cartagena, Colombia.

A city filled with cobblestone streets, vibrant colors, and enough energy to wake Abraham Lincoln, Cartagena is near the very top of my list of favorite cities in the world.

The weathered walls of the Old Town section of the city act as a shield, protecting the legacy and history of Cartagena. And beyond the Old Town walls lie the tropical beaches and vast sea, offering a welcomed contrast of laziness to the liveliness of what lies within the walls.

In Cartagena, it is easy to get by on a low budget. Just walking around the streets of the city is exciting enough that you could spend a week wandering the same streets and still not tire of it.

There are cheap food options on nearly every corner (although, take it from me, it is entirely possible to survive on all the different offerings of ceviche served throughout the city and nothing else) and you can find locals selling beer out of coolers for impossibly cheap prices.

Cartagena can be extraordinarily cheap if you want it to be.

But there is a side to Cartagena that can rival places like Paris and Milan in terms of luxury. Luckily, for Erin and I, it was time for my penultimate luxury experience on the venture.

From the moment we checked into our Relais & Châteaux Boutique Hotel, Casa Pestagua, we were treated like celebrities. In fact, we were told upon check-in, as we were being poured glasses of freshly popped champagne, that American actor Owen Wilson had just checked out of the room we would be staying in, and it was, without question, the best room in the hotel. Not that any of the 11 suites and deluxe rooms are anything but exceptional.

Casa Pestagua is often referred to as "the most beautiful house in Cartagena." In the seventeenth century it was owned by the Count of Pestagua, a very rich and powerful aristocrat.

When you walk into the courtyard of Casa Pestagua you will be staring into what looks to be secret chambers of ancient times. I was half expecting to see Cleopatra and Marc Anthony relaxing on the lounge chairs next to the royal blue swimming pool underneath the open sky.

In the daytime you could be in the courtyard catching rays while being served hand and foot by the most attentive staff in South America. In fact, it took everything in my power to not order a bushel of grapes each day and have someone feed them to me. In absolute serenity you can float the day away surrounded by the tropical vegetation of the surrounding garden.

In the evening you could eat dinner in the same courtyard and enjoy the exotic flavors of their French cuisine.

Then, in the morning, you can start your day with a visit to the spa for a "ritual" or body treatment by one of their world class expert masseuses.

After two days of pampering that we quite frankly didn't deserve, we realized that we had spent nearly all of our time in Cartagena within the confines of our Boutique Hotel.

It was time we explored Cartagena.

Reminiscent of Havana, Cuba, the streets of Cartagena are filled with color, dancing, and music. Everywhere you turn there is a new local "amigo" waiting to sell you something or show you around their beautiful city and become your new best friend/tour guide.

And because we were in Cartagena on a luxury budget, we were not shy about saying "Yes," to the vast majority of offers we received.

"Senora, you want to buy this hat? You would look hermosa (beautiful) wearing it," the hat seller said to Erin.

"Yeah, sure. I'll take a hat," she replied .

"Do you have any for men? I'll take one too. A blue one if you have it," I chimed in, making for the easiest sell the aging hat seller had likely ever made.

And with that, we had a new hat-selling best friend following us around, shooing away any other locals that wanted to try to sell us stuff we didn't need."

He followed us all around the city, telling us "He can find *whatever* we are looking for," dragging out the word *whatever* as much as he could.

"We are not looking for anything," I replied, "We are just walking. Maybe we will buy more from you tomorrow."

PRO TIP: NEVER tell a Colombian hat seller that you *may* buy another hat from him tomorrow. You may think that the odds of running into each other the next day would be astronomically high, but I can assure you, they are not.

We finally ditched the hat man by diving into the most expensive looking restaurant we could find and sitting down at their bar, knowing he would not be allowed to follow us in there. In addition to giving us some much needed space from the hat-seller, it also gave us reprieve from the obnoxiously hot mid-day Cartagena sun.

After eating more orders of fresh seafood ceviche than one should ever eat we headed back out on the streets.

We took approximately ten steps when we walked past a tour company selling day trips to Islas del Rosario, a tropical paradise just 20 miles away. The combination of the slideshow presentation that was being conducted on a television on the side of the road, which flashed dazzling photos of the Caribbean bliss, and the friendliest salesman on the face of the Earth, made it all but guaranteed that Erin and I would make the purchase.

Chalk up another easy win for Cartagena salesmen.

And while you're at it, chalk up another Cartagena best friend that insisted we look into the other tours he had to offer and follow us around to "protect us" from other locals trying to sell us things we didn't need.

Again, we dipped into the next fancy restaurant we could find, and spent enough time in there until we thought our new "tour-selling best friend" had moved on to someone else, resigned to the fact that he would see us for the tour tomorrow and likely sucker us into buying something else from him.

When it was safe to exit the restaurant we decided to make our way to the Old Town walls and have a walk around its border.

We initially passed the steps that led to the part of the wall you could walk on, so I hoisted myself up effortlessly onto the four-foot ledge.

The same can not be said for Erin.

After about three failed attempts to hoist herself up onto the wall, I was way too much in a fit of hysterics to help her. Luckily, for her, there was a local guy that just so happened to be standing on the wall right next to where she was making a fool out of herself, who was more than willing and able to help her.

"Dame tu mano, senorita, (give me your hand, miss)" said Fabian, a young twenty-three year old local, in his seductive Colombian accent.

Without so much as a wince of effort he grabbed her hand and pulled her up the wall in the most superhuman way possible.

But this isn't what made Fabian a real hero. What made him into the legend that he still is today, is the fact that he was selling ice cold beers for about $1 USD. It is hot as hell in Cartagena, and this young, buff, guy appears out of nowhere, yanks Erin up a wall, and then looks at me and says, "You want cerveza? Buy one get one free."

We would buy ice cold beers from him, then would take a tour of a museum, or a stroll around part of the wall and circle back to him. And every time we saw him, he would say the same thing… "You want cerveza? Buy one get one free."

He was to me, as I would imagine Clarence the Angel was to George Bailey in *It's a Wonderful Life;* a savior. Just when I thought I couldn't go on living anymore in the Cartagena heat, he would appear and refresh us with ice cold beers.

We repaid Fabian by inviting him to our Boutique Hotel and buying him, what I would imagine to be, the most fancy meal he had ever had.

After dinner, we parted ways and told him we were going on an island tour the next day, but would come and visit him as soon as we got back to Old Town. We promised we would miss each other very much for the next 16 hours, hugged until it became awkward, and then ushered him out the door.

You won't be shocked to learn that the next morning as Erin and I walked out of our hotel to head to our island adventure, the very first person we ran into was our hat-selling best friend from the day before.

He followed us all the way to our tour, and while we didn't get suckered into buying anything from him, we did make the idiotic mistake of telling him, "We will be back at 5:00 p.m. maybe we will buy something then."

Amateurs, I immediately thought, slapping myself on the forehead.

Our island cruise went off without a hitch and we spent the day basking in the hot Colombian sun and being pampered by our island hosts.

But as we were heading back to Cartagena five hours later, our "tour selling best friend" said to us, "You are from the USA. You have HBO GO?"

Before I could think why he would be asking us this, I yelled "Of course."

You both must love *Game of Thrones*. Am I right?"

"Why yes, we do," we both replied.

"Perfect. Let us all watch the premiere of the final season together tonight," he said, with a smile stretched across his entire face.

"Ummmm, ok," we replied, each wondering how the hell we were going to get out of this mess, but deep down both knowing damn well, we weren't.

When we got back to the tour company there were two people waiting outside. Fabian, our beer-selling best friend, waiting with a cooler full of beers for us, and of course, our hat-selling friend that promised he would find us when we returned.

"Ugh, come on, follow me," I said to them both.

"Where are we going?" Fabian asked.

"To our 5-star Boutique Hotel to watch *Game of Thrones*. You better behave yourselves," I said, staring all three of them in the eyes one at a time.

When we walked into our hotel we were greeted with champagne by the staff. "We have missed you both very much the past two days, why haven't you been staying here all day," the main server, Juan, said to us.

"Well, we had to at least see some of Cartagena while we were here," I said, feeling sad that they were worried about us not thinking the hotel was doing an adequate job at tending to our every needs.

"Can we get three more glasses for our friends," Erin said, pointing to the Scarecrow, Tin Man, and Cowardly Lion that were lingering behind us.

"And when do you get off?" I added. "Grab the staff and let's all watch *Game of Thrones* in the courtyard."

"I am very sorry, but we do not have HBO," said the head server, devastated, again, thinking that he could not serve our needs.
"It's OK," I responded, "I have HBO GO."

It took one look from Erin before I edited myself while standing in the Relais & Chateaux 5-star hotel that Owen Wilson had just checked out of two days before, and I had dragged three strangers from the streets into, "Well... *my parents* have HBO GO," I admitted, "But I have their password."

34. Peru - Low Budget Does Anyone Want Anything?

You never realize just how quickly a year can go by until you have spent it traveling around the world. Physical and digital calendars and clocks are replaced with intangible phrases such as "Does anyone have any idea what day it is?" or "Is it still February?" and "Well, the sun is setting, so it must be around time for dinner, right?"

But Erin, who had to return to normal life, and needed to keep better track of such seemingly mundane knowledge, casually kept reminding me of things such as "You know it is May 1st, did you call your dad for his birthday?" or "Isn't it crazy that Memorial Day weekend is in just two weeks?" and most traumatizing of all, "I can't believe I have to fly home tomorrow! And you have to meet your college roommate in PERU!"

"Please don't remind me about Peru," I would say every time she mentioned the country.

Not because it was my final destination on a venture around the world and after I left I would have to return to reality. And not because I wasn't looking forward to having my college roommate, Shane, fittingly join me for my last few weeks of the best year of my life, in fact it was his idea/fault I was heading to Peru in the first place. But it is WHY he is making me meet him in Peru that I was dreading heading there, but more on that story in the next two chapters.

First, I must make it from Colombia to Peru…

Because Erin and I extended our stay just about everywhere we went, (we never really can get enough of a good thing,) I had to make last minute adjustments before I left Colombia in order to meet Shane in Lima, Peru on time.

This meant, among other things, I had to cancel my original plans of taking slower means of transportation, such as busses through Ecuador, which would have allowed me to spend a week exploring the country along the way.

Ecuador may look moderately sized on a map or globe, but a bus journey from its northern border, Colombia, to its southern border, Peru, is quite an adventure.

So, even though I was technically leaving Colombia and entering Peru on a low budget, believe it or not, the cheapest way to make the journey was to fly. The two and a half hour journey would save me a weeks worth of traveling through Ecuador in which I would stop and explore every place that the bus stopped, spending money on accommodations, food, drinks, activities, and God knows what else.

In order to save time and money I decided to book a $86 dollar flight from Bogata, Colombia to Lima, Peru.

Erin and I shared a taxi to the airport and said our goodbyes, although to be perfectly honest it wasn't overly emotional for three reasons…

1. Seeing as I, too, was returning home after Peru, we would see each other in just a few weeks.

2. We were a smidge "under the weather" from watching the *Games of Thrones* premiere with half of Cartagena when our flights took off. It is hard to care

about anything when you are hungover, except of course wanting desperately to die.

3. After traveling with a loved one for a month, you are way more than at peace with getting a bit of space from them.

But, in all honesty, within the past year, Erin accompanied me to eleven countries and through my own stupidness or hers, afforded me with a plethora of stories to write an entire anthology of books. Her presence was a gift beyond words.

Anyway, enough of the sappy stuff. Let's talk about the *MIS*adventure of Mr. Brightside while he was taking an otherwise brief, and more importantly cheap, flight to Peru.

I boarded the plane at exactly 11:00 a.m. which sounds like the perfect time to board a flight, right?

You get to sleep in a bit, you can have some breakfast and coffee in the morning without scarfing it down while driving half-asleep to the airport; it's perfect.

11:00 a.m. boardings, I love you.

That is, of course, unless your flight was scheduled for 7:02 a.m. and you arrived at the Bogota airport promptly at 5:50 a.m..

In which case, 11:00 a.m. boardings suck.

Erin boarded her flight and we waved dramatically at each other as if one of us were heading to the front lines of World War III and may never see each other again.

Then, as my flight continued to get more and more delayed, my frustration level began to grow. So I decided to leave my gate and take a stroll around the airport. Much to my delight, about twenty-five steps from my gate was the VIP lounge for Priority Pass holders. If you are even a semi-frequent traveler and you are not a Priority Pass card holder, you are making a terrible life choice.

A Priority Pass card will allow you access to certain VIP lounges in hundreds of airports around the world. If it is the morning, there is typically a free breakfast for you to enjoy. In the afternoon, free lunch, and in the evening, free dinner.

You have comfortable seating and places to charge your devices. Some Priority Pass lounges even have showers for you to enjoy while you wait for your flight. And almost all of them have some sort of bar with free booze.

Technically speaking I was on a low budget, but thanks to my Priority Pass, I had breakfast and drinks and VIP access for free.

I have been to a hefty amount of Priority Pass lounges around the world, but the one in Bogota, Colombia was far and away the best I have ever experienced. It is the Sandals Resort of Priority Pass, and I vowed to myself to make a return trip to Bogota simply to spend more time in the airport lounge.

After hours spent enjoying the luxury of the lounge (for free) it was finally time for me to board for my flight to Lima.

Through no fault of my own, I now had a few drinks in me, and decided to allow myself ONE drink on the flight to keep my buzz going.

My seat was 1B, meaning I was in the front row of the plane and in the middle seat. In my opinion, the front row middle seat is by far the most underrated seat in all of travel.

You are the first to deboard the plane. You have all the legroom you would desire. You do not have to bother anyone in the aisle seat if you need to go to the bathroom. And you do not need to get up if the window seat person needs to use the bathroom. If you are a solo traveler, and not sitting in the middle seat in the front row, you, too, are making terrible life decisions.

So I plopped down into my seat and introduced myself to my neighbors. I immediately learned that neither of them spoke a lick of English, so I aborted the mission of making new friends and put in my headphones.

Moments later, we were in the air for our short flight to Lima. In this case, "short," is a relative term. After traveling around the world for 11 and a half months, a two hour and thirty minutes flight is akin to taking a ride around a neighborhood block.

Before we had even made it into the air, both of my neighbors were fast asleep. I made a mental note of this, to remind myself to try not and wake them as I was ordering my one and only beer I was allowing myself to drink on the flight.

About twenty minutes into the flight the flight attendant came by with the cart. I was, obviously, her first stop as I was in the front row. The guy next to me in the aisle was still asleep, just I said to her, in my quietest whisper, "what kind of beer do you have."

She responded with such a cacophonous boom that I would be shocked if someone in the bathroom at the back of the plane didn't hear her. She was so loud, in fact, that she even startled me, who was *anticipating* a response, so you can imagine how startled my sleeping neighbors were.

"SENIOR, WELL WE HAVE PILSEN CALLAO BEER, CUSQUENA BEER, AND CRISTAL BEER. WE ALSO HAVE CUSQUENA CERVEZA NEGRA I THINK. LET ME CHECK (she checks,) YES, SENIOR WE DO HAVE CUSQUENA CERVEZA NEGRA."

By now the entire plane was awake and I could feel every single eye directed at me. My neighbors awoke, and the people across from the aisle were staring, having been distracted from their book, phones, and whatever else they may have been doing.

"Great," I whispered, even more softly, hoping this would set a standard for how loud the rest of our interaction needed to be, "I will have the Cusquena. The regular, not the Cusquena Negra."

My face was beet red and I felt horrible about disturbing my seatmates from their sleep, so I asked each of them if they wanted anything. They both politely declined.

"Oh, COME ON! Get something!" I insisted.

"OK. I will have a glass of wine," the lady in the window seat said in Spanish (I only know that because the roaring loud flight attendant handed her a glass of wine.)

"Cusquena Negra," said the aisle seat man, having been traumatically woken from his slumber just a few seconds prior.

"CUSQUENA NEGRA, SI," screamed the flight attendant, loud enough for the people still waiting in the airport to hear.

Thanks to all the commotion now the three people across the aisle from us were shooting death glares at me.

"Do you guys want anything?" I asked, more to stop the awkward glares than to be nice.

I was sure they would say something like "no thank you," or "oh, that is so kind of you, but totally unnecessary," but they didn't.

Their responses…

"Si," "Si," and "Si."

So I ended up having to buy the entire front row of the airplane a drink.

"I will come back and collect your money after I finish the rest of the plane," said the flight attendant.

"OK," I said, "you take cards, right?"

"Oh no. Only cash," she said. "We said that in our announcements before we took off."

I panicked for a few seconds thinking I did not have any Colombian money before I remembered that I had three large denomination bills in Colombian pesos (100,000,) the equivalent of about $30 USD each, a total of about $90 USD.

The flight attendant came back about 15 minutes later and said 120,000 pesos, so I handed her two 100,000 pesos. She looked at me, then screamed loud enough for my hard of hearing grandmother to hear back in Rhode Island, "OH NO, SENIOR. WE

DO NOT HAVE THAT SORT OF CHANGE. ANYTHING SMALLER?"

"Nope," I said. This is all I have, showing her the one final 100,000 peso in my otherwise empty wallet.

"Sorry. No change," she hollered.

"Ummmmmmmmmm" I said for about a solid minute, before adding, "So what do I do?"

"YOU BUY ONE MORE ROUND AND I WILL CHARGE YOU JUST THE $300,000," she whispered. And by "whispered," I mean spoke in a normal voice, as to not alert the entire plane she would give me a discount if I bought six additional drinks, five of which for complete strangers that I had never spoken to.

"Is there really no change at all?" I asked, finding it hard to believe.

"No senior," not many people order alcohol on this flight. And we do not have change for a bill that big," she replied, this time screaming again.

"Whatever. Fine. Buy another round. Here take the money," I said, a tad annoyed.

The five strangers then received another glass of wine or can of beer, nodded their heads at me, and one after one said "Gracias," before returning to their books, phones, and in-flight magazines.

I sat in complete shock that within thirty minutes I bought 12 drinks on a plane, resulting in a bar tab that exceeded the price of the actual flight, and immediately started making tweaks to my low budget itinerary to save even more money for my first four days in Lima, Peru.

35. Peru Moderate Budget
I'm Ziplining, Baby!

Not for a lack of trying, my three best friends from college and I typically only manage to reunite once, maybe twice a year. Shane, Kristen, Neil and I always manage to get together towards the start of every new year, seeing as three of us celebrate our birthdays within just a few weeks of one another.

After a typhoon of hugs and kisses, and Christmas, New Year's and birthday well-wishes, the four of us gather to make fun of each other, enjoy some cocktails, reminisce about the old days, and, well… make fun of each other some more.

But the January before my venture began, we had another topic of interest to discuss; my trip around the world.

"Anywhere in the world," I said to them at the dinner table, "You name the country, and I will put it in my itinerary and will meet you there."

Kristen and Neil all but ignored me, with Kristen saying something along the lines of "OK sure, let me just tell my husband and kids that mommy is going to spend some time in India drinking marijuana infused milkshakes and try her luck at sleeping in the jungle with the hopes of not getting malaria. No big deal."

And Neil would say something like, "OK, let me quit my job and make plans to meet you in six months when we all know that prissy little Ryan is going to be back home crying for his mommy and daddy the first time he sees a spider."

But Shane, after pointing at me and laughing maniacally at both Kristen and Neil's response to my kind-hearted gesture of inviting them said, "Let's do it!"

On my second day of college, before classes had even begun, I remember sitting at my desk in my dorm room, carefully sharpening my pencils, and getting a jump start on the required semester reading. I was carefully labeling all of my notebooks and color coding them, pairing all the notebooks with a designated folder that would accompany it to each of my classes. I brushed up on some math facts, and even woke up early to go for a stroll in the courtyard to watch the sun rise for the first time of my college career[5].

Then, as I was just about to head to the library[6], I heard the door to my suite slam open and saw what looked to be the Partridge Family stroll through my dorm. Leading the pact, a skinny platinum blonde wanna-be skater boy with a skin-tight, sleeveless undershirt, (for lack of a better term and for the sake of posterity, a wife-beater.) His mother, little brothers, little sister, big sisters, and friends all joined in unceremoniously interrupting my study session[7], and moving his pretty-fly-for-a-white-guy ass into Rhode Island College, Thorpe Hall, Suite Q.

This, my dear readers, was Shane, the man who twenty-one years later whole-heartedly proclaimed that he would, indeed, join me for part of my venture around the world.

"If you are serious," I said to Shane, which is rare because in the twenty-one years I have known him, neither him nor I have ever

---

[5] None of this happened, and I was actually still in bed, hungover, but I don't think my parents know how to use footnotes.
[6] Bathroom to vomit
[7] Drafting of a letter to the Dean explaining that I would need to drop out of college before it even started because I couldn't handle it.

been serious one single solitary time, "You name the date, the country and whatever you want to do, and I will be there."

He didn't need time to respond… "Peru. May. Let's hike to Machu Picchu."

I didn't need time to respond either… "Shucks[8]," I whined, "But let's do it."

Seeing as I was busy planning 11 and a half months of travel, I left the planning for the entire two weeks in Peru up to Shane. And it wasn't until a few weeks before we were scheduled to arrive in Lima that he sent me a link to tickets he just purchased for a Machu Picchu adventure.

Without even looking at the details I followed the link, whipped out my credit card, purchased the adventure tour, and sent him the confirmation.

I wasn't sure what we were doing, but knowing Shane, I was sure it would be something that involved not being able to shower for at least a week.

After my four days on a low budget in Lima, Peru in which I basically starved myself to death due to me being a complete moron and buying half the passengers on the plane a drink on the way there, I met up with Shane in Lima where we would head to Cusco, Peru for four days of moderate living and whatever else he had planned for us.

Shane has been rambling on and on for years about how much he wanted to hike the Inca Trail to Machu Picchu, so I was

---

[8] "Fuuuccckkkk," was what I actually said, but I don't think my grandmother knows how to read footnotes.

mentally prepared for that exhausting grand finale to take place in Peru. What I wasn't mentally prepared for, and still not mentally healed from, is what he had planned for us the days leading up to our Machu Picchu hike.

It turns out that Shane's lovely wife, Sarah, has just as much aversion to heights as I do, so she was more than happy to hand Shane over to me for a few weeks so he could get as many traumatizing, hair-raising, excursions out of his mid-life-crisis ridden body as possible.

Never one to back down from something that scares the living shit out of me, I agreed to all the activities that were provided in our all-inclusive package, which unfortunately just so happened to fit in with my moderate budget days do to the fact that we stayed in low budget accommodations with cold, dripping water and one sheet that functioned as both "warmth" and "protection from whatever animals were flying/crawling/scurrying around us."

There were six brave adventurers in our group for the three-day excursion, Ryan and Kristen, a lovely young married couple from Texas, Carlijn and Eline best friends from The Netherlands, myself and Shane.

Ok, fine, there were five brave adventures that had to babysit me for the three day adventure and me.

Day one involved a ride in a van that took us on a harrowing journey up the most narrow, curve-filled mountain in the southern hemisphere. Throughout the nearly two-hour drive I heard the gang yelling things like "Oh my God! That is the most beautiful view I have ever seen," or "Quick! Someone take a picture of that," or "Wow, people live their entire lives and never see a view that spectacular."

I, however, was not yelling any of these things, because I was wearing a sleeping mask and humming as loud as I could while plugging my ears so as not to see how close we were to plunging to our deaths, nor hear the intricate details of how high up in the mountains we were.

Eventually, after an eternity spent holding myself hostage, the car stopped and the doors opened. I took off my mask and will begrudgingly admit the view was astonishing. We were at the top of the world looking down at the peaks of smaller mountains as if they were miniature building logs. Besides the excitement of my fellow travelers, there was not a sound to be heard, and not another soul in sight. It was actually quite peaceful.

But that brief moment of serenity quickly vanished into thin air as the guides took the cover off of the cart we were pulling behind us and unloaded seven bicycles, shut up the van, and drove away leaving only the six of us and one guide behind.

"Where is the van going?" I asked in a panic.

"Back down the mountain, our guide told me."

"When is he coming back to get us?" I cried.

"Never. We must meet him at the bottom," he laughed.

"No way. There is not a chance in hell that I am getting on a bike and riding it down that mountain. When you said we were going to ride bikes, I thought we were just going to ride around for a bit up here, perhaps in a nice, flat, grassy knoll, and then get back in the van."

"No. We must go. Get on," the guide yelled.

"Come on, Ry, we will go slow," Shane yelled.

"You have no choice now," Caroijn laughed. "You will be fine."

I physically started to dry heave, which made everyone laugh at me even harder. But they were right, apparently there was nothing I could do about it now.

I hate bikes, and hate heights, and hate Shane, and hate my new friends, and hate my tour guide, and absolutely fucking HATE Peru, I said out loud to myself as I strapped on my helmet, got on my bike, and began braking my way down the mountain.

"Yeah, Ryan! YOU GOT THIS!" screamed Ryan and Kristen.

"I AM SO PROUD OF YOU!" yelled Eline, who was already almost out of sight, and not at all concerned about looking where she was going.

"I HATE YOU ALL!" was all I could say.

"Especially YOU, Shane," I added.

"Love you, bud," is all he kept saying, through fits of hysteria.

As it turns out, if you brake the ENTIRE time you are riding, don't look anywhere besides the small patch of road in front of you, and stay all the way against the mountain and never move closer to the edge of the cliff, regardless of where cars are driving, there are *BRIEF* moments where you may feel the thrill of this type of adventure.

Once you get your brain to stop thinking about plunging to your death, only to have your remains never recovered, it may even be, dare I say, a tiny bit fun.

A few times I even worked up the courage to take my hands off the brakes and cruise down the mountain at a less snail-like pace.

Occasionally, I even caught glimpses of my friends waiting ahead for me, but every time I got near them I screamed for them to keep going because the last thing I needed was to be distracted by my own screams of *I hope you all fall off the cliff for making me do this. Especially you, Shane!*

At one point I was, in fact, so far behind them that another entire group caught up to me.

Three Aussies whipped by me, and a fourth, after catching up with me and seeing how slow I was going, yelled to his friends, "You lads go on, I am hanging back here with this mate."

"Fuck this, huh?" were his first words to me.

Finally, I said out loud without making eye contact or looking anywhere besides the pavement directly in front of me, *someone that gets me.*

Brian and I drove side by side for nearly an hour, eventually seeing both of our groups up ahead, and both of us yelling "GO! WE DON'T WANT TO SEE ANY OF YOU!"

Then we would ride another half-hour or so, as the process kept repeating itself.

About three hours after I began my death defying ride, Brian and I heard something like a *hummmm* whizz by us.

"What was that?" I asked him, frantically.

"I don't know, you look, I am not taking my eyes off the road, mate," he said.

"Let's both pull over and stop and look," I said, as I effortlessly slowed my roll to a complete stop, took off my helmet, and looked down the road at what had just flown by us.

"It couldn't be," I said to Brian, "Are you seeing what I am seeing?"

"Is that a baby?" he shrieked.

"What kind of LUNATIC would ride a bike down this with a small child strapped to their back?" I huffed in disbelief.

"I suppose we are being awfully cautious, maybe we could go a little bit faster. What do you think?" Brian suggested.

"Well, I guess if that mom thinks it's safe enough for her child, I guess we could go a little faster and see what happens."

No sooner had we rounded the corner after deciding we were going to be more adventurous did we see all of our friends and both of our vans waiting for us.

"FINALLY," about 16 people all yelled at once, in about as many different accents.

"Can we PLEASE get out of here, we have been waiting all day for you two," said Brian's friends.

"I HATE YOU ALL!" Brian and I yelled at the same time.

I got in my van and Brian got into his and as it turns out both of our groups were heading to the same accommodations.

"I am proud of you buddy," Shane said, in his gentle, most compassionate, sincere voice that only a longtime friend can say.

"Screw you," I said, looking at the window, thankful to be alive.

"I got you a beer from the store while we were waiting for you, I knew you would want one."

Without saying a word, I leaned over and gave him the most subtle, insincere kiss on the cheek that a person could.

We drove back to our lodging and departed the van. As we were walking back to our rooms, the guide yelled to us, "ONE HOUR WE WILL MEET BACK AT THE VAN."

Now what, I said to myself, too traumatized to even speak it out loud.

It turns out that our next adventure was white water rafting, and much to everyone's surprise, I was totally comfortable with that.

They had all made bets about who I was going to punch in the face first upon hearing the news, but the joke was on them because I am not afraid of white water rafting and made sure to make that abundantly clear to each and every person in the van.

"I have been white water rafting many times. I even went white water rafting on *the Nile River*," I dramatically said 75 times on the half-hour long ride to the river.

"Yes, we know, you have told us 7...38...74 times, someone would respond each time."

Still, I was happy to not give them something else to laugh at.
For now.

White water rafting went off without a hitch, and I made sure to point and laugh as hard as I could each time anyone showed any fear about the rapids tossing us overboard, or the raft flipping over, forcing us to gasp for breaths any time the rapids allowed us to come up for air.

"AMATEURS, THE WHOLE LOT OF YOU!" I would maniacally scream every time we almost drowned.

Gosh, I can be a complete jerk sometimes. I still, to this day am amazed I have a single friend.

We got back to the lodging a few hours later and showered for dinner. When he was finished eating, our guide told us to meet at 6:00 a.m. the next morning at the van for ZIP-LINING.

I threw down my fork, and without looking up from my plate could feel Shane looking at me with a stupid grin on his face, and said, "Don't say a single word."

By 6:20 a.m. I was already paralyzed with fear. We were still in the offices of the Zip-Lining company being instructed on how to not die on the ziplines.

Our group was larger now, about 12 of us in all.

I had been zip-lining before, but all of those times were child's play compared to this. This was zip-lining through mountains and canyons. There was one zip-line that itself was over ONE MILE LONG.

I insisted at every zip-line we got to that I needed to go first because I could not stand the fear of being on top of the platform without being attached to the cord. To the people I did not know, I must have seemed like the most self-absorbed human being of all time.

"I am sorry, I am just terrified and need to get this over with," I would say, at each platform.

They all agreed I could go first. I do not think it was because they felt bad for me, but because they didn't want to have to listen to me moan and cry for a half-hour every time we had to wait in line.

After six zip-lines we got to a wooden bridge that separated us from the final ULTIMATE zip-line.

The bridge in *Indian Jones and the Temple of Doom* was more secure than this bridge, even after one side of it was chopped and it was dangling from the cliff, dropping everyone not tied to it to their deaths.

I demanded Shane to go first to make sure it was safe.

He graciously accepted this task and said "I will go slow, you stay behind me."

After he was five rungs in, I took my first step, with a line of about 15 people behind me.

"How are you doing, pal?" he yelled, as I was only on my second step.

"DON'T TALK TO ME!" I yelled.

He said "OK, sorry," and started walking faster.

"STOP, GET BACK HERE! YOU ARE WALKING WAY TOO FAST! DON"T YOU DARE LEAVE ME!" I screamed.

"Sorry, I thought you wanted me to leave you alone," he politely responded.

"SHUT UP, LEAVE ME ALONE!" I screamed back.

This poor guy could not win.

It was, without a doubt in my mind, the most scared I have ever been in my life.

I ordered him to go ahead and cross the bridge. I wanted to take my time, and if I ended up falling through the bridge to my death, the last thing I wanted to see before I died was his face and hear him yelling "WHAT DID YOU DO, YOU IDIOT?"

"IS ANYONE BEHIND ME?" I yelled.

"Yes. It is me, Carlijn," I heard, "but do not worry. I am fine. You go slow and take your time."

I will not even begin to string together the profanity that was coming out of my mouth during the trek across the bridge, but if you care to hear it, feel free to contact Shane, as he has plenty of videos of me once he got to the other side.

Finally, after the scariest seven minutes of my life, I was safely on the other side. I turned around to cheer on my friends, but there was no need to. All 11of them finished within seconds of me, meaning I was holding up the entire group of people. I was prolonging what I am assuming was something they most certainly did not want to be prolonged.

I apologized profusely to all of them for going so slow and for whatever they heard that came out of my mouth.

I all but ran to the final zip-line to be able to finally get this traumatizing day over with and was shattered when I saw there was still a line from the group that left earlier than us.

I scanned the line to see how many people I had to wait through before I could end this.

The line was too long, and we were at our highest peak of the day. If I had to sit and think about this mile-long zip-line any longer I feared I would literally drop dead of freight.

I asked the line if there was any way I could cut them because I needed to get down. I may or may not have lied and told them it was an emergency.

"Of course, mate."

"Oh, no. Hope everything is OK, Go!"

"Absolutely, dear."

These were some of the responses I heard.

Then I heard a tiny muffled voice that sounded like a talking German Cabbage Patch Doll say in the cutest voice you have ever heard, "You can go in front of me too," It was in perfect English, despite the thick German accent.

I looked down and saw the same little girl that zipped past Brian and I strapped to her mother's back riding down the mountain the day before.

She had her blonde-as-a-bus yellow hair pulled back into the cutest little pig tails you have ever seen, and was wearing a harness that could have fit on a chihuahua.

I looked down at her. She could not have been more than four years old and weighed less than 30 pounds.

She was fearless.

I looked over to Shane and he looked more nervous than I have ever seen him look in our twenty-one years of friendship.

"You are not going to cut this little girl," he mouthed to me, his eyes pleading with me.

I looked at him, looked at the mile long zipline ahead of me, and looked back at him, his eyes still bugging out of his head like a moron.

I shrugged my shoulders.

Then I looked at the mother who was also staring at me, and finally down at the little girl.

I bent down so I was staring her right in the face, and spoke as slowly and dramatically as I would if I was speaking to a deaf person, who also happened to be nearly blind, but needed to read my lips to be able to understand what I was saying.

"THANNNNNNNKKK YOUUUUUU SOOOOOOO MUCCCCCHHHHH, SWEEEEEETHEART."

I patted her on the head, and without looking back at Shane told the worker, "I am ready to go. Clip me up, please."

And within seconds, I was peacefully drifting on a mile long zip-line through the mountains of Peru with not an ounce of fear in me. I was zip-lining my way straight to the safety of the cabin and going to buy myself as many Peruvian beers as it would take in order for my friends to wait in that terrifying line on the mountain's edge.

36. Peru Luxury Budget
The Final Venture

After a third of a year traveling around the world in luxury, the time has come for my final luxury days of my venture, and the final days of my year-long trip around the world.

But this final stint in "luxury" would be far different than my previous experiences. There would be no resorts or spas, no jacuzzis or massages, and no private islands of any kind.

In fact, these final days in luxury were going to be quite the opposite of what I deem as luxurious.

Instead, we would be dwelling in the picturesque town of Aguas Calientes, Peru, at a small, modest hotel with gorgeous views of the Urubamba River and even more breathtaking views of its surrounding mountains.

This may sound luxurious to you, but that may change when you find out how we got to Aguas Calientes…

We walked.

Hiked, actually.

And not on freshly paved roads or lush green fields. We hiked, with all our gear, along the treacherous cliffs of the Inca Trail from Ollantaytambo to the base of Machu Picchu.

For two nights and three days we walked. And walked. And walked.

We walked 40 kilometers (25 miles,) the vast majority of which was up steep, sickeningly narrow Andean mountain paths at an altitude that was too high to even comprehend.

The cost of this adventure included a few nights of hotel accommodations, various meals along the way, tour guides to make sure we didn't die (and in my case hold my hand for a few hours each day,) and a final night at the aforementioned hotel once we arrive at the base of Machu Picchu.

It also included admission to a thermal hot springs swimming area near the end of the trek, should you be fortunate to actually make it there without dying.

We left our hotel at 3:30 a.m. and made our way through the darkness on foot up a long, straight, uphill road. There was no mistake, this road was UPHILL. But according to the guides, this was very much the "flat part" of the voyage.

I believe it was around 3:35 a.m. when I first said to my companions, "I have made a huge mistake."

I have been on multi-day hikes before, including a five-day hike down and up the Grand Canyon, which also traumatized me for life, but this was something altogether different.

For about an hour we carried on up the "flat part" until we reached a wooded area with a sign in front that said, "Welcome to Inca Trail."

Behind the sign, a slim dirt path that was so uphill it was nearly vertical. I looked up at the top of the hill the exact same way I looked up at the top of the Eiffel Tower when I was standing beside it. Straight up.

"What the shit is that path for?" I said.

"That is where we start going up, replied the guide."

"There is no way we are walking up that. You are crazy if you think I am walking up that," I cried to our guide that spoke limited English, but probably understood what I was saying based on the crazed look in my eyes. Surely he has seen this panicked look on other people's faces, as he had probably hiked up this trail more times in his short life than I have brushed my teeth.

He responded by pointing to the top of the mountain and said three words…

"We go. Now."

There was no arguing with this guy. So I put my head down, moaned like a child that couldn't get his way, and walked.

As I began the trek upwards, I was standing vertical for about four steps before it no longer became possible. After that I was "walking" up the mountain the way a two-year-old would walk up a flight of stairs to their bedroom. Left foot. Left hand. Right foot. Right hand.

I turned around to make sure everyone else was also climbing up in this ridiculous fashion.

They weren't.

So I stood back up and attempted to walk like a normal adult again, and promptly began falling backwards.

Well, I have already embarrassed myself enough these past four days, I said to myself, *let the bastards laugh at me,* and got back down on all fours.

This continued for about twenty minutes before I heard the guide yell from up front.

"We break soon. We are almost at the Monkey Temple."

"Monkeys scare me, and I do not want to be around them if at all possible," I said to Shane, "But this better be a very long break."

Gasping for air and covered in dirt from head to foot, I had finally arrived at our first break of the day, the Monkey Temple. I am assuming I look more frazzled after two hours than most people that make this trek look after the third full day, but it was physically impossible for me to care any less how I looked at that point.

The woman at the temple that worked/lived/probably has never been anywhere else but that Monkey Temple on the side of a massive mountain in her entire life, greeted us with a warm smile and a bowl of popcorn.

I thought it was quite odd that of all things she had popcorn, but was too tired to question it.

I walked right by her, gave a quick wave, tried to utter the word "Hello," but was too out of breath, and collapsed to the ground.

"Are we almost there?" I cried.

It was day one.

And the sun had not even fully risen.

Growing up, monkeys were always my favorite animals. I admired their carefree attitude, playfulness, and the way they randomly bounced from here to there. In every stupid journal prompt in English class in school growing up, whenever the inevitable question arose of "If you were an animal which animal would you be and why?" I always said "A monkey, because they are fun and funny and do whatever the hell they want."

The teachers would always respond with something like…

Ryan, great effort, and yes, I could see you as a monkey if you were an animal because you are a fun and funny kid. And yes, you do always do whatever you want. But next time, please remember to reword the question in all of your journal responses.

C+

But the older I became and the more first hand experiences with monkeys that I was confronted with, I came to realize that I do not like monkeys, and if I was to suddenly be forced to turn into a monkey, I would not be happy. I would choose a sloth, because they are so laid back. Or a hyena, because they like to laugh all the time (*The Lion King* taught me that.)

In fact, I am basically the polar opposite of a monkey. I have seen monkeys be extraordinarily mean to people in my days. In South Africa I saw a monkey/baboon whatever the hell it was, walk into my sister-in-law Justine's family's house, jump up on the kitchen table, reach into their fruit bowl and steal the bananas out of it and make sure they knocked as much shit over in the process as they could before they exited the house.

I would never do something like that.

In Uganda I would frequently see monkeys attack small children that happened to be holding food in their hand until the children dropped their food and ran away, screaming with fright.

Again, that is something else I would never do. Especially to a poor child in a Ugandan village that was probably planning on eating that chunk of meat for their next 12 or so meals.

And in India, at the Taj Mahal, I have seen tourist place their shopping bags on the ground to gawk at the beautiful building and take about 75 selfies, and while doing so, a family of monkeys would jump in from out of nowhere, pick up their bags, and jump away with them, never to be seen again.

I swear, they are horrible.

And don't even get me started about the 2009 Oprah Winfrey interview with the poor woman whose pet monkey decided to eat her face right off of her head.

So we are at the Monkey Temple and the entire crew went on a tour of the establishment. I chose to use my time a little more wisely and caught up on more important things, such as breathing and sitting and mentally preparing for the next leg of this nightmare.

Way too soon the crew came back to join me and my blood pressure rose thinking it was already time to head back out. But to my delight, the guide told us to take a seat on the couches and relax. He then brought over two bottles of liquid, looking very much like bottles of tequila.

It was about 7:00 a.m. and the sun had just risen.

These people sure know how to get the party started, I thought to myself, *maybe I could live up here. It is one of the most beautiful views I have ever seen. And I do enjoy popcorn.*

But when the host got a bit closer to us and showed us the bottles, we noticed something floating in both of them. Something that looked very similar to a gigantic dead snake.

"There is no way those are dead snakes floating in those bottles, right?" I whispered to my Australian friends.

"No way, mate," one replied encouragingly.

"And you see in these bottles that we have dead snakes floating in them," the host said, almost on cue.

On second thought, I said to myself, *maybe I can't live up here. It's not even THAT beautiful, anyway.*

"This is a Jungle Snake drink, a drink that is homemade and very popular in this part of Peru," said our host. "You are very lucky to be able to try it," he said, after seeing the look of shock on our faces.

"Why is there a snake floating in it?" just about every one of us yelled at the same time.

"The venomous snake is known to add extra flavor to the drink," said the man.

"VENOMOUS!" we all gasped, clutching our chests.

"Yes, but you have no need to worry, the venom is killed by the ethanol in the drink," the host said calmly.

"Can we use the term "alcohol," instead of "ethanol,"" I joked, making the entire group let out a much needed laugh. "Try some of this snake venom alcohol drink sounds safer to me than try some of this snake venom ethanol drink."

"In addition to adding flavor," our host said, ignoring my hilarious joke, "The snake is also known to represent wisdom and the underworld, which leads some to believe that this snake drink has healing abilities. Who wants to try first?"

No one volunteered, so I stood up, walked to the man and said "Well, every single part of my body is hurting at the moment, so who am I to pass up a drink that has healing abilities?"

The man poured me a shot of snake drink and I sucked it back before I even gave it a second thought.

"The eleven of you may be better at hiking and biking and zip-lining and walking than me, but I am better at drinking snake venom ethanol," I said, laughing in their faces.

We all have our strengths.

One by one the rest of the crew tried the shot, and handed me any snake venom ethanol that was left in their shot glass that they did not finish.

"At this rate, I am going to be the healthiest man in all of South America," I joked, before turning to the mountain's edge and screaming into the vast canyon, "I AM THE HEALTHIEST MAN ALIVE!"

I forgot we were at a monkey temple and my screaming apparently woke all of the damn monkeys out of their slumber and made them all start freaking the hell out. Monkeys were jumping all over the damn place, which in turn startled all the parrots that were hanging around too.

Since I created pure chaos, and ruined everyone's relaxation time, my guide said "OK. Maybe we should go now."

"Good job, Ryan," said one of my Dutch friends, "Now our break is over and we must hike again. You should probably go now and get a headstart on all of us," she joked.

At least I hoped it was a joke.

So we said our goodbyes to our Monkey Temple host and began the life-threatening hike along the edge of the cliff.

"How long until our next break?" I asked our guide, "You know, just so I am mentally prepared."

"You do not want to know, sir," he replied, walking past me.

Uh-Oh, I thought.

Talk about a buzz-kill.

What seemed like months later, as I was panting for breath at the back of the line, and trying not to look anywhere but the ground straight ahead of me, because if I took one wrong step I would have plunged to my death, I heard the guide say "Food break. We stop now."

Finally, I thought, *about damn time we took another break.*

I looked around and wondered where the hell we were going to eat. We were on a cliff and hadn't seen another human being or building since we left the Monkey Temple.

Once I finally caught up with the rest of the group I noticed they were all huddling around something. I pushed my way through the huddle and saw that they were all staring at a nest.

"Who wants to try a termite?" the guide asked.

"This better be your idea of a joke," I said, hoping that right around the corner I would see a Hard Rock Cafe Inca Trail or something.

"We will eat real lunch in an hour," said our guide, "But first, who wants to try a termite?"

I could tell we were going to stand on that damn cliff until someone tried one and appeased the man.

"Ugh, give me the fucking termites," I said, grabbing a pinch-full from the nest and popping them in my mouth. "Can we get a move on now?" I said, as I walked on, leaving behind a group of stunned hikers, and a guide that was both flabbergasted and beaming with pride.

Almost to the minute, after another hour of horror, we walked up to a log cabin style building and six picnic tables.

It was time for a real lunch, and a much needed break.

After lunch we had about three hours left to hike for the day, and the only thing that got me through the absolute terror of the cliff walk, and the scariest part of the adventure, was the fact that I had found out, over lunch, that Ryan and Kristen from Texas were, like me, huge *Survivor* fans.

I went into a near black-out state rambling every fact that I know about *Survivor* and don't think I shut up for the entire three hours[9].

That night, I slept like a baby, and instead of having nightmares about cliff-walking, I dreamt of being on *Survivor* and having beers with Jeff Probst after winning my record-breaking fifth reward challenge in a row.

The majority of the second day of hiking was nowhere near as traumatizing as the first, and not as difficult of a climb. After all, we already spent an entire day hiking up a damn mountain, how much higher could we possibly go?

We made stops along the way which included a lovely break where our guides whipped out a guitar and played for us as we joined in on sing-alongs. Just when you think that "Wonderwall" by Oasis couldn't possibly be any better, try listening to it while in the middle of the Inca Trail performed by local tour guides. I couldn't help but think that maybe this song that was released in 1995 was just finally making its way to the Inca Trail after all these years.

That thought made me both extraordinarily happy and sad at the same time.

While we were all singing along, we had some locals paint tribal war paint on our faces. I didn't quite catch what the purpose of this was, but who was I to complain about anything that would extend our break even further.

---

[9] This fact was indeed confirmed to me by about nine very annoyed people that never wanted to hear the word "*Survivor*" ever again once we finally got done with our day one hike.

We then hiked another six million miles[10] and ended up at our final stop of the day, the thermal springs.

I was way too lazy to change into a bathing suit, so I simply jumped in the springs in my boxers and began floating away in thermal bliss.

I didn't even have time to introduce myself to anyone else in the springs before dark clouds rushed in overhead. They were the blackest clouds I had seen since the end of the world happened when I was in the Sahara Desert ten months prior, and we quickly exited the springs, gathered our belongings and made our way to a van that was waiting to take us to our accommodations for the night.

A vehicle. An actual moving vehicle with wheels was going to transport us. I have never been happier to be squeezed into a seven passenger van with twelve people in all my life.

Our final day was our shortest hike yet, and this time I was leading the pack. The thought that we were nearly done with our hike stirred up something in me that made me hike like I was Daniel Boone's mentor and taught him everything he knew.

I was basically running, yelling back to Shane and our friends things like "Hurry up, slow pokes," and "My grandmother could hike better and faster than you losers."

Again, one of the biggest mysteries of our time is the question of how the hell I have any friends.

I rounded a corner, humming the tune of Davy Crocket to myself, and suddenly, in the distance, was a sight I will never

---

[10] This is a rough estimation based on how my body felt.

forget. The thing we had hiked days to see. The sight that I nearly died multiple times trying to get to. Machu Picchu.

The end of the hike, and the end of the journey was in sight.

Even though it would still take over an hour to get to the town of Aguas Calientes, I didn't care. Unless I had the worst luck of all time, and a boulder crashed down on my head and flattened me like a pancake, I had made it.

I had survived the hike. I survived the monkeys. I survived the snake venom-ethanol cocktail. I had survived the Inca Trail.

An hour later we entered the beautiful little town of Aguas Calientes, and each checked into our own hotels. Shane and I entered our small, yet moderate hotel room, with the beautiful views of the Urubamba River and its surrounding mountains. It was the smallest room imaginable, with a queen bed and an old, random wooden chair. Its bathroom provided cold running water with almost non-existent shower pressure and a sink that would clog upon each use.
But to me, it was the most luxurious room I had stayed in all year long.

We awoke again at 3:30 a.m. the next morning, and made our way in the cold darkness to the base of Machu Picchu to begin our trek up the 1588 steps to the entrance. This would be my last venture on a year long journey that took me through 29 countries, 5 continents, and more towns and cities than I can count. 1588 steep, excruciating steps is all that separated me from accomplishing everything I set out to achieve. And you can bet your bottom dollar I would count every single one of them out loud.

Acknowledgements

First I would like to thank my loved ones that rented me a party bus to take me to the airport to begin my journey around the world. William Jacobson, Cory Jacobson, Justine Jacobson, Joy Fidrych, Mark Fidrych, Renee' Fidrych, Steve Congdon, Kristen Federico, Steve Morrone, Lisa Reed, Kris Reed, and Jill Page (and Rachel and Sean Doyle for the idea.) Thanks to you, and all the libations that were supplied on said bus, I was sobbing like an idiot for the first five hours of this experience.

An additional "Thank you," goes out to my beloved grandmother, Minnie Ravenelle and nephews, Andrew Jacobson and Liam Jacobson. They are the reason this entire thing was able to happen as it was their job to stay home with my hyperventilating mother, and make sure she didn't call the border control to prevent me from leaving the country.

Next I want to thank all my travel companions that joined me in a portion/portions of my travels. Brendan Kenahan (The Azores), Daniel Casey (Portugal, France, Andorra, Spain, Morocco), Erin Burke (Morocco, Italy, Albania, Montenegro, Hungary, Kosovo, Macedonia, Serbia, Panama, Colombia), Paul Brayman (Germany), Kelly Page (Croatia), and Shane Roche (Peru). You were all a welcomed familiar face in a sea of strangers and I'll forever be grateful to have shared part of this experience with you.

Also I would like to thank all of the people I met along the way. Strangers quickly became best friends, and because of all the kind, caring, and welcoming people I met throughout the year, I never felt alone or lonely.

Thank you to all of my family, friends and co-workers that helped support me in this journey, either through "going away gifts," or simply through all of your emotional support and confidence in me that I could complete this journey.

Thank you to Jacquelyn Lawton, Erin Burke and Linda Cafferty who did countless edits to make sure my horrible spelling skills went undetected and unnoticed.

Thank you to the band The Killers for the thousands of hours I used your music to drown out the sounds of loud roommates, neighbors, Indian traffic, annoying swindlers, and ear-piercing modes of transportation.

Thank you to all the accommodations, restaurants and excursion companies that offered me free or discounted experiences in order to be able to write this book. Your generosity is very much appreciated.

Thank you to you, the reader, for taking the time to complete this book and for not judging me too hard for still acting like a college student[11].

And finally, thank you to my parents, William and Michelle, for always supporting me and taking care of all my business back home as I traveled the world. I apologize mom, for all of your sleepless nights. And I apologize even more to you dad, for all of mom's sleepless nights.

---

[11] Middle school student.

About the Author

Ryan Jacobson is a middle school English teacher born and raised in Westerly, Rhode Island where he currently resides. He has been to 38 countries and counting. When he is not traveling the world, he is likely planning and preparing for his next adventure, visiting a local vineyard, or talking endlessly about *Survivor* or The Killers to anyone that will listen. This is his debut book.

To read blog posts of all of these adventures and more, and to see pictures of events depicted in this book, visit his website at www.venturetwelve.com/the-book

Made in United States
North Haven, CT
17 August 2022